AMISH QUILT
PATTERNS

AMISH QUILT
PATTERNS

Rachel T. Pellman

Illustrated by Craig N. Heisey

Good Books®
Intercourse, Pennsylvania 17534

Acknowledgments

Design by Craig N. Heisey.

We wish to give special recognition and thanks to Rebecca Haarer for her help on this project.

We also wish to give special thanks to the following persons for their gracious permission to picture their quilts on the cover of this book:

Center photo — Sunshine and Shadow, William B. Wigton.

Other photos, clockwise from top left — Bow Tie, Rebecca Haarer; Broken Star, William and Connie Hayes; Fan, Diana Leone; Center Diamond, privately owned; Log Cabin, William and Connie Hayes; Ocean Waves, Judi Boisson Antique American Quilts, New York; Roman Stripe, The Darwin D. Bearley Collection; Double Wedding Ring, Judi Boisson Antique American Quilts, New York; Double Nine-Patch, Jay M. and Susen E. Leary; Tumbling Blocks, Rebecca Haarer; Baskets, Rebecca Haarer; Bars, Jay M. and Susen E. Leary.

Photograph Credits

Photos on cover and on pages 7 and 15 by Jonathan Charles.

AMISH QUILT PATTERNS
Copyright ©1984 by Good Books, Intercourse, PA 17534
International Standard Book Number: 0-934672-23-7
Library of Congress Catalog Card Number: 84-080652

Table of Contents

Introduction	6
Amish Quilt Patterns	8
Total Quilt Assembly Design	16
Border Application Design	17
Center Diamond	18
Sunshine and Shadow	20
Bars	22
Multiple Patch	24
Irish Chain	26
Log Cabin	28
Double T	32
Stars	34
Jacob's Ladder	36
Baskets	38
Fan	40
Ocean Waves	42
Roman Stripe	44
Tumbling Blocks	46
Rail Fence	47
Bow Tie	48
Robbing Peter to Pay Paul	50
Shoo-fly	53
Monkey Wrench	54
Carolina Lily	56
Crown of Thorns	59
Bear Paw	60
Pinwheel	62
Garden Maze	64
Railroad Crossing	66
Double Wedding Ring	68
Diagonal Triangles	71
Drunkard's Path	72
Tree of Life	74
Bachelor's Puzzle	78
Rolling Stone	80
Quilting Templates	82
Circular Feather	83
Pumpkin Seed — Variation 1	87
Triangular Rose	89
Ivy Leaf	97
Feather Border	99
Grapes with Leaves	109
Fiddlehead Fern	111
Tulip	115
Pumpkin Seed — Variation 2	117
Cable	119
Dogwood	125
Floral Border Design	125
Readings and Sources	127
Index/About the Author	128

Introduction

The magic of antique Amish quilts has begun to capture admirers everywhere. This book offers patterns, step-by-step instructions, and color suggestions for reproducing many favorite antique Amish quilts.

Why the Interest in Antique Amish Quilts?

Perhaps it is the simplicity and peace visible in the lives of the people who made them that has made their quilts so fascinating. Perhaps it is the combination of energy and restraint in these quilts' simple geometric patterns that give them such broad appeal. Perhaps in a modern, fast-moving techno-logical age people grasp for links with the past to find stability. Whatever the impetus, there are increasing numbers of people interested in Amish quilts.

Many old quilts from the larger Amish settlements of Eastern Pennsylvania and the Midwest have already been purchased from private homes by museums and collectors. The transition happened slowly at

first but soon the Amish com-munities were ravaged by "door knockers"—persons who stopped randomly at Amish homes offering to buy any old quilts. Some homes had old quilts stolen from them while the family was away at church. That understandably made the Amish community uneasy so some owners decided to sell their quilts before they were stolen. Some wanted to sell but wished to wait until the market drove the prices higher. Others wanted to keep their quilts and got weary of questions. But most did not understand the unusual demand.

Within the Amish community, values and commitments are taught and passed on to the next generations through a way of life. Consequently, for the Amish a tangible symbol of their past is not important or sought after because their basic values are firm and generally not losing ground. In fact, for them a new quilt seems a more appropriate wedding present than an old one. And so, many old quilts left homes with their sellers happy to have the cash instead.

For those outside the Amish com-

munity, these old quilts stand as symbols of the past. They speak of a time of long family evenings, winter leisure and handcrafted works of love. Their bold shapes and dark vibrant colors show stability and freedom within specific limitations.

Many persons continue to search for these works of art from the past. But the quilts are increasingly hard to find. **AMISH QUILT PATTERNS** attempts to provide for the next best thing—a good reproduction. It is not possible with modern dyes and fabrics to duplicate the deep warm colors produced by natural dyes. Some strikingly true reproductions have been made with the use of old fabrics. But it is also possible to come close to the old look with careful attention to fabric selection, pattern, scale, and quilting designs. This book attempts to provide those patterns in the proper scale and with easy-to-follow instructions so that anyone can make one of these prized quilts.

We have enlarged these patterns in the proper proportions to accom-modate today's bed sizes.

Sunshine and Shadow, 1940s. Cotton, crepe, 88 x 86. Lancaster Co., Pennsylvania. The People's Place, Intercourse, Pennsylvania.

AMISH QUILT PATTERNS

Good planning is the most basic rule in successful quiltmaking. It will minimize many frustations!

You should know before selecting your fabric which quilt pattern you are going to make, how many colors you will need to complete your choice, and which colors or color families you want to use. Since it is difficult to visualize a grouping of colors and fabrics in a quilt when working with either large bolts or small swatches, it is helpful to sketch a scale model of the quilt onto graph paper and then use crayons or colored pencils to fill in the appropriate colors.

Making a Model

You can get an even more accurate color representation by purchasing small amounts of the fabrics under consideration and cutting them into tiny patches to cover the appropriate areas on the scale model. This is especially helpful when working with those patterns using large geometric shapes. It becomes more tedious when working with patterns involving small patches. Despite that,

it is a very beneficial exercise since it allows the quilter to see in advance whether one fabric is lost or dominant among the others. If, for instance, you are trying to emphasize a particular design

within a patch, the surrounding areas will need to provide adequate contrast so the design pattern will stand out. This dimension can be achieved with light and dark fabrics or by the use of contrasting colors.

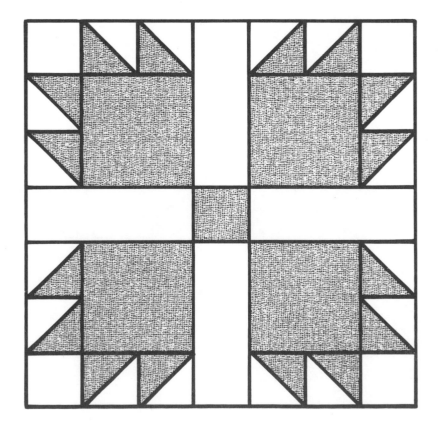

Choosing Good Fabric

The quality of a quilt is only as good as the quality of each of its components. Therefore, it is essential to choose high quality fabrics for quiltmaking.

Lightweight 100% cotton or cotton/polyester blends are ideal for quiltmaking. In addition, 100% cottons have a dull finish, making them similar to the old fabrics. (Cottons blended with synthetics tend to have more lustre or sheen.) The fabric should be tightly woven so it does not ravel excessively. If you check its cut edges and find it frays easily, the fabric will be difficult to work with, especially in small pieces.

Test it for wrinkling by grasping a handful and squeezing firmly. If sharp creases remain when the fabric is released it will wrinkle as you work it and will not have a smooth appearance especially if it is used in large sections on a quilt. It is wise to wash all fabrics before using them to preshrink and test them for color fastness.

Selecting "Amish" Colors

Most Amish quiltmakers did not understand the science of color selection and combinations. They followed their intuitions and used what was at hand. In the past and today, Amish homes are bare by most American standards. Walls are generally painted a plain blue or green. Floors, if carpeted at all, are usually covered with handmade rag rugs. Very little upholstered furniture is used. In short, these people, because of their commitment to simplicity, have traditionally given very little effort to coordinating room decor and accessories. The same is true of their clothing. The Amish style of dress is prescribed by the church. They are not concerned about the latest styles or fashion colors. These matters have simply never applied to the Amish way of life. Consequently they are not bound by the surrounding culture's sense of what is proper and what is not.

This freedom from the dictates of society's norms is evident in the color schemes of antique Amish

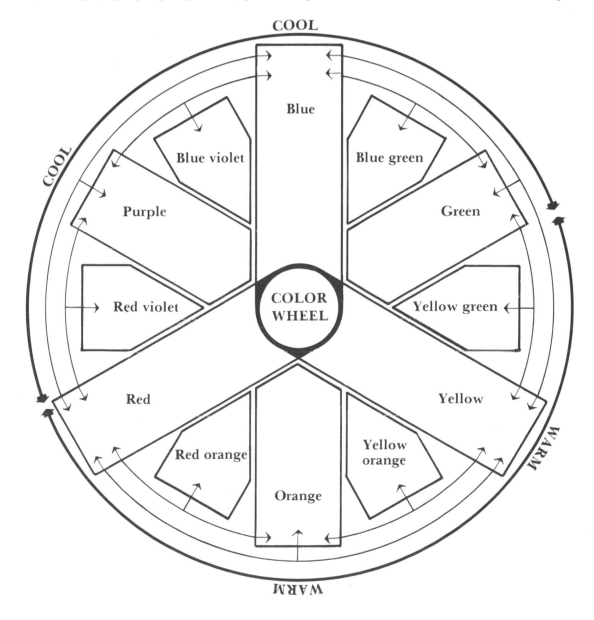

quilts. Frequently, the colors which color theory describes as complementary often appears together in Amish quilts. Likely the makers never *knew* they had selected complementary colors, but they could *see* that those colors brought out the best in each other.

Many Amish quilts have accents of black and red, a combination that decorators recognize as a boost for many color schemes. When Amish women emptied their scrap bags they didn't work from a basis of scientific knowledge. They just chose their fabrics in relation to each other. Many times the result was a dramatic color scheme that stands up well today.

It would be unfair to create the impression that all Amish quilts were masterful in color. There are many that are less than pleasingly co-ordinated. But if you would like to capture the best in antique Amish quilt colors, you will likely be most successful if you try to forget what you know about color and begin with a fresh new approach.

There are several guidelines you might follow. The fabrics used in antique Amish quilts are almost always solid colors. Printed fabrics seldom appear. The oldest, most traditional Amish quilts come from eastern Pennsylvania, specifically from the Amish of Lancaster County. This earliest settlement tends to be more conservative than some of the groups who later migrated to other areas. The clothing colors of this group used only part of the spectrum of the color wheel avoiding those colors known as warm colors—bright reds, red orange, orange, yellow orange, yellows, and yellow green. The "cool" colors—burgundys, blues, purples, and greens were the colors permitted for clothing and also used in quilts. Therefore, these more conservative, traditional Amish quilts reflected their community's standards and used a myriad of colors, but only those

within the boundaries of that "cooler" spectrum.

Antique Amish quilts from areas outside the eastern Pennsylvania communities were often more daring in their colors. Yellows and oranges appear frequently in midwestern quilts and those from Pennsylvania counties other than Lancaster. However, these colors are used in conjunction with the traditional darker hues. For example, it is extremely unusual to find an Amish quilt using only a scheme of earth tones.

Play with colors in several arrangements before you make a final decision. See how they stand in reference to each other. Some colors highlight one another and others dull them.

Try, as much as you can, to approach your color selection in an uninhibited way. The closer you can get to that approach, the more likely it is that you can create a quilt that looks authentically Amish.

Don't Forget Black

To approximate "Amish" color choices, you will do best by using colors of varying intensities and shades. And don't forget black. Black, although very dark, can be a spark of life in a color scheme. Several shades of black may be more interesting than only one. The varying shades that appear in old quilts happened because they were often scrap quilts. So substitutions were often made for fabrics that ran out. You should not be afraid to try substituting one or several similar fabrics instead of using the same one throughout the quilt.

Figuring Yardage

Aside from the quilt back, one of the areas requiring the largest amount of fabric on pieced quilts (particularly antique Amish patterns) is the border. The border looks best if it does not need to be pieced. Therefore, its fabric should

be purchased adequately so as to run the entire length of the quilt. Any fabric remaining along the edges after the borders are cut can be cut into patches for the top.

Be sure to calculate seam allowances when figuring yardage. And it is a good idea to remove all selvages from fabrics before cutting, so allow for that when calculating the width of the fabric you need. Most quilting fabrics are 45 inches wide.

Since most quilts are wider than that, you will likely need to piece the back of the quilt. When calculating yardage requirements, remember that the back should be two to three inches larger than the quilt top to making quilting easier, so add that additional fabric for ease in quilting. You should buy enough fabric so that it can run the full length or width of the quilt without being pieced. Then buy as many lengths or widths as you need to cover the quilt back. Remember to calculate for seams when stitching the back together.

Figure the total yardage you need for patchwork pieces by calculating the amount of fabric you need per block, and then multiply that by the number of blocks of that color in the quilt. Again, remember to allow for ¼ inch seam allowances on all sides of each patch. If there will be fabric left from the borders and back from which patches can be cut, delete that amount from the calculated requirements.

Planning Borders

Border treatments vary greatly on quilts. They may be seen as a way to quickly increase a quilt's dimensions to an adequate size, or they may be the frame that highlights the quilt pattern. Sometimes they achieve both at the same time. At any rate, a border should not come as an afterthought. Plan your quilt dimensions with the border in mind. Many Amish quilts have wide, elaborately quilted borders.

The important factor is that the borders be in proportion to the interior pattern of the quilt. This will vary from pattern to pattern.

Pattern Templates

The accuracy of a template will make a monumental difference in whether a quilt fits together or not. Templates should be very accurately traced onto a material that will withstand repeated outlining without wearing down at the edges. Cardboard is not appropriate for a template that must be used repeatedly. More durable materials are plastic lids from throw-away containers, the sides of a plastic milk or bleach jug, old linoleum scraps, or tin. (If tin is used beware of sharp edges.) Sandpaper may be glued to the back of the template to keep it from slipping as you mark the fabrics.

Before you cut all the quilt's patches, cut enough for just one block by using the new template. Then assemble the patch to check for accuracy. If changes are required (perhaps the corners don't meet), adjust the template and try again. Always test the template by assembling one block before cutting fabric for an entire quilt top.

Templates may be made with or without a seam allowance, depending on the method of marking, cutting and piecing preferred by the quilter.

Marking Patches with Seam Allowances

This method requires that the template be made with a ¼-inch seam allowance on all sides. When traced onto the fabric, the marked line is the cutting line. The seam line is ¼-inch inside the marked line. The advantage of this method is that if you work with a very sharp scissors, you can trace the outline on the top layer of fabric, but then cut through several layers of fabric at the same time. The

disadvantage is that when you begin stitching the patches together, you will need to accurately guess the exact location of the ¼-inch seam allowances so that the corners of the patches meet accurately.

Marking Patches without Seam Allowances

This method requires that the template be made the actual size of the finished patch. When traced onto the fabric, the marked line is the stitching line. The cutting line must be imagined ¼ inch outside this line. The advantage here is that you have a tracing line to stitch along, almost guaranteeing accuracy in piecing. The disadvantage is that each patch must be marked and cut individually. With this method you cannot stack and cut multiple layers of fabrics. Each quilter must choose which of these methods works best for her/him. The important thing is to maintain accuracy by whatever way is most comfortable.

It is extremely important to be precise in marking and cutting. A very minute mistake in either step will be multiplied many times over when you try to assemble the quilt. Ultimately, you want to have a smooth flat quilt top. To achieve that, the individual pieces must be precisely fit together.

Marking Fabrics

There are many ways to mark fabrics. You may use a regular lead pencil to trace the template. However, on some fabrics, especially dark fabrics, the markings are very difficult to see.

There are several pencils designed especially for quilters. Some of these make markings that are soluble in cold water allowing for easy removal of markings. Some pencils make markings that disappear after a certain period of

time. That works well if the pieces marked are used before the time elapses. Whatever you choose, be sure to follow the manufacturer's instructions for its use.

Every quiltmaker should have a good pair of sharp fabric shears. The longer the blade of the scissors, the greater the chances of cutting a continuous straight line. The scissors must be sharp all the way to the point to cut well-defined corners.

Piecing

You may piece a quilt in either of two ways: by hand or by machine. Hand-piecing is a more time-consuming and laborious process and most quilters today choose to piece by machine. However, when very small pieces are used and when several points need to meet, hand-piecing is the most precise and exact method. This way also allows the quilter to work on the project anywhere rather than being tied to a sewing machine. If hand-piecing is done, borders and the sashing between blocks can still be stitched on the sewing machine to save time.

The hand-piecing technique is very simple. You must pin the patches with their right sides together and with their stitching lines perfectly matched. Using a fine sharp needle, stitch with short running stitches through both layers of fabric. Stitches must be straight, even, and tight to achieve an accurate and strong seam. Check stitches periodically to be sure they are not causing puckering. Put an occasional backstitch in with the running stitches to tighten the seam without creating puckers. At the end of the patch, backstitch and knot the thread before clipping. Open the patches and check the seam for precision.

When piecing, always begin by assembling the smaller patches and build them on to the larger pieces to form the quilt block. Combine patches to form straight sewing lines whenever you can. You will want to avoid having to set in squares and triangles if at all possible since stitching around corners requires utmost care to prevent bunching and puckering. When setting in is required, as in star patterns made from diamonds, it is important to stitch the patches that need to be set against each other only to the ends of their stitching lines, and *not* proceeding to stitch through their seam allowances. The seam allowances must be kept free to fit against the seam allowance on the piece being added.

There are two ways to set in a corner. One is to start at the outer edge of one patch, stitch its full length (stopping at the seam allowance), pivot, and proceed along the other edge. The other method is to begin stitching along the edge at the center or inner corner. Stitch from the inner corner to one outside edge and then go back to the corner and stitch the remaining edge. Practice both methods and use the one most easily completed for you.

Machine-piecing is obviously a lot faster. The procedure is basically the same as hand-piecing but the stitching is done by machine. Pin patches together accurately and watch carefully that they do not slip when going through the machine. In machine stitching there are no knots so it is important to backstitch whenever beginning or ending a seam.

When joining units of patches to each other there is always the problem of what to do with the seam allowances. Seam allowances are a noticeable menace in two situations: one, if quilting needs to be done through the seam allowances making small stitches virtually impossible; and two, if a seam allowance of a dark fabric is visible underneath a lighter fabric. It is generally a good idea to lay all seam allowances in the same direction. However, if this will create either of the above problems, make an exception and lay the seam allowance the opposite way.

Preparing to Quilt

Much of the magic of old Amish quilts is in their quilting. They are lavished with quilting designs, leaving few open spaces. This tiny, intricate quilting is essential in reproducing the look of an old quilt. Full-size quilting templates are included in this book.

Marking those designs on the quilt top can be done in a variety of ways. See "Marking Fabrics" on page 11 for information on quilt-marking pencils. Remember to mark with something that will not rub off easily as quilting requires having hands against the surface. On the other hand, the markings must be something that is completely removable when the quilting is completed so that unsightly lines do not remain.

If you work with fabric that is light enough to see through, the easiest way to mark is by tracing. Outline the quilting designs on paper with a heavy magic marker. Lay the fabric to be marked, wrong side down, on top of the quilting design. Trace, with a fabric marker, over the lines to stitch.

Although this method is easiest, many fabrics used in these quilts are too dark to see lines through the fabric. Therefore, the design must be traced in an alternate way. This can be done by cutting very thin slashes at intervals on the quilting template. This creates a dot-to-dot effect with the slashes. The template is then laid on top of the right side of the fabric and the lines are traced onto the quilt top.

Since templates are used repeatedly it is wise to make them of a material more durable than paper. Cardboard or thin plastic are suitable.

Straight lines or crosshatching can be marked by laying a ruler on the fabric and tracing along both sides. On large areas, a chalk line can be snapped across the quilt.

When patches are being outlined, no marking around them is necessary. Simply quilt close to the seam to emphasize the patch.

Quilting is both a descriptive word and an action word. To quilt means the process of stitching 3 layers of material together to form a heavier whole. The finished stitches, often done in decorative patterns, are called quilting.

A quilt is a sandwich of three layers: the quilt back, the lining or batting which adds insulation value, and the top which is often pieced or appliqued. The three layers are held together by the quilting stitches.

Making Tiny, Even Stitches

Quilting is a simple running stitch. It is done most easily and durably with quilting thread since it is heavier than regular thread and more able to withstand the repeated pulling through the three quilt layers. Quilting needles are called "betweens." These needles are shorter than "sharps" which are considered the normal handsewing needles. Betweens come in various sizes which are identified by numbers. Most quilters use a size 7 or 8 to quilt. Some quilters prefer the even smaller size 9 needle. The best way to choose a needle size is to try several and then use the one that seems most comfortable.

A thimble is a must for quilting since the needle must be pushed repeatedly through three fabric layers. The thimble should fit snugly on the second finger of the hand used for pushing the quilting needle.

To begin quilting, cut a piece of quilting thread about one yard in length. Thread the needle and make a single knot at the end of the piece. Then insert the needle through *only* the quilt top about 1 inch from where quilting will begin. Pull the thread through to the knot. Gently tug on the knot until it slips through the fabric and is lodged invisibly underneath the top. This will secure the quilting thread at the beginning. With one hand underneath the quilt and the other on top, push the needle through all three layers until the hand underneath feels a prick. That indicates that you've been successful and stitched through all the thicknesses! (Experienced quilters develop calluses from this repeated pricking!)

Then with the thimble on your upper hand, tilt the needle upward. Use your lower hand to push up slightly from underneath. As soon as the needle point appears again on top, reinsert it through the layers again. Continue this process until three to five stitches are stacked on the needle. Finally, pull the needle and thread through the fabric to create the quilting pattern. The stitches should be snug but not so tight as to create puckering. Continue the process of stacking stitches onto the needle until the thread is used. When the length of thread is nearly gone, do a tiny backstitch to secure the thread. Insert the needle again through only the top layer and make a stitch the length of the needle, away from the quilting design. Pull the needle through the surface and snip the thread with the long stitch left buried underneath the quilt top. Thread the needle and begin again.

The goal to strive for is tiny, even stitches. And they come only with practice! Initially, concentrate on making straight *even* stitches, without worrying too much about their size. Try to have the stitch length be the same on both the top and bottom of the quilt. Holding the needle straight is crucial for

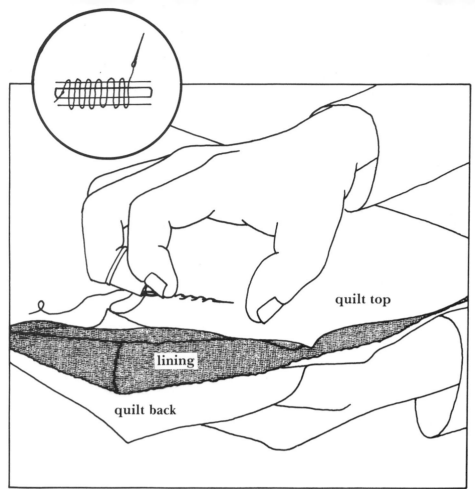

A quilt is a sandwich of three layers — the quilt back, lining or batting, and the quilt top — all held together by the quilting stitches.

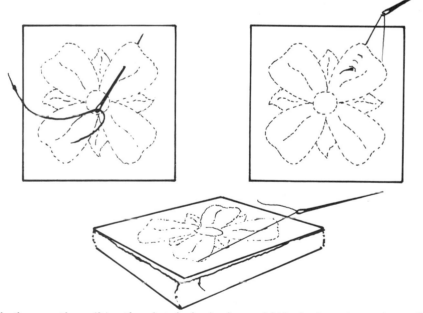

To both secure the quilting thread at the beginning and hide the knot, insert the needle through **only** the quilt top about 1 inch from where the quilting will begin, pull the thread through to the knot, and gently tug on the knot until it slips through the fabric and is lodged invisibly underneath the top.

achieving straight stitches. Then after you have mastered evenness, try to decrease the size of the stitches.

When quilting curved lines, do not try to stack as many stitches on the needle before pulling it through. No more than two stitches in the needle at a time are best for executing smooth, even curves.

The type of batting or lining used in a quilt will affect its finished look. Much of the batting available today is polyester and has a much puffier quality than the linings used in antique quilts. Cotton batting is available from some quilt supply shops. Another option is to use a thin sheet blanket or something similar to add weight and insulation value but retain the flat appearance of the old quilts. These thinner materials also make close even stitches more possible.

Putting the Quilt in the Frame

In order to achieve a smooth, even quilting surface, it is necessary to stretch all three layers of the quilt in a frame. This creates a taut surface conducive to quilting. The most traditional and probably most effective frame is the type that is large enough to stretch the entire quilt out at once. This allows for even tension over the whole quilt. These frames are generally used at quiltings when several persons work on the quilt at the same time. The disadvantages of such a frame are its size and lack of mobility. Since the entire quilt surface is exposed, the frame obviously requires that much floor space. Also, once the quilt is stretched in the frame it should not be removed until quilting is completed. That usually means that the space is occupied for an extended period of time. Many quilters do not have the space required for such a frame.

Another type of frame accommodates the entire quilt at once, but most of it is rolled onto a long rail along one side of the frame. Only about a three foot length, along the width of the quilt, is exposed for quilting. As that area is completed the quilt is rolled onto the opposite rail until the entire quilt is finished.

Still smaller frames are available for quilters with very limited space. These look like giant replicas of embroidery hoops which allow for the quilt to be quilted in small sections. A very important procedure before using this type of frame is to baste the entire quilt together through all 3 layers. Basting should begin at the center and work out towards the edges. Doing this assures that the layers will be evenly stretched while quilting and avoids creating puckers during the quilting process. But when you quilt, do not quilt over the basting stitches because this makes them extremely tedious to remove later.

Binding the Quilt

The final step in finishing a quilt is its binding. The binding covers the raw edges along the four sides of a quilt. Bindings, particularly on antique Amish quilts from Pennsylvania, are generally wider than bindings found on many other quilts.

Since the edge of a quilt receives a lot of wear, the binding is often done with a double thickness of fabric. It is not uncommon for bindings on old quilts to have been machine-stitched in place although hand-stitching is less obvious.

Bindings can be done in several ways. One of the easier methods is to cut strips of fabric that measure four times the width of the finished binding. These strips can be cut either lengthwise or cross-wise on the fabric grain. Length-wise strips do not need to be pieced, but piecing on a binding is not very obvious and can be done without minimizing the beauty of the quilt.

The binding strips should measure about one inch longer than the quilt on two of its parallel sides. And on the other two sides, the binding strips should be as long as the quilt's

width (or length) plus one inch, plus the double finished binding width from the other two sides.

Fold the binding strips in half, wrong sides together, so that both raw edges meet. Trim any excess lining and backing from the quilt itself. Pin the shorter two binding strips against the two parallel edges of the quilt top's width, with the raw edges of the binding flush with the raw edges of the quilt. Machine stitch in place using a ¼ inch seam allowance. Open the seam so that the folded edge of the binding is now the outer edge of the quilt. Sew the remaining binding strips onto the other two sides of the quilt extending out to the folded edge of the attached binding strips. The binding is now folded in half again so that the previously folded edge goes around to the back and covers the seam made by attaching the strips. Handstitch the binding in place. Fold corners under so that no raw edges are exposed.

Another method of finishing a quilt, less commonly used on old Amish designs, is to simply wrap excess border fabric from the top, bottom, and sides of the quilt around to the back where it is stitched in place. Or the extra backing fabric may be wrapped forward over the raw edges to the front where it is stitched in place on the quilt top. Most old Amish quilts use a cut binding. It is frequently in a color which contrasts with the border and is new to the color scheme of the interior of the quilt.

After the binding is completed, you may want to initial and date the quilt so that it can be identified by future generations. If you sign and date with embroidery that should probably be done on a lower back corner. Or if you quilt in the initials and dates that, too, is usually done in a corner.

Bars, 1910-20. Cotton, 78 x 73. Lancaster Co., Pennsylvania. The People's Place, Intercourse, Pennsylvania.

Total Quilt Assembly Diagram

Diagram 5.

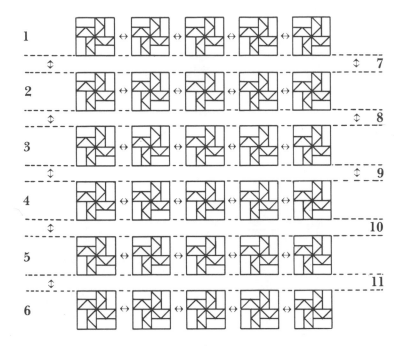

Diagram 6.

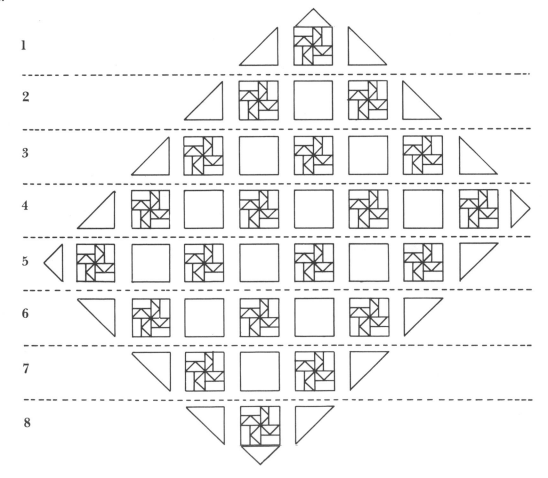

Border Application Diagram

To obtain correct border length, measure length of edge to which border will be applied. Border widths are given with each pattern. When corner blocks are used, sew them to the ends of the last border pieces and then add the border and blocks as a complete section.

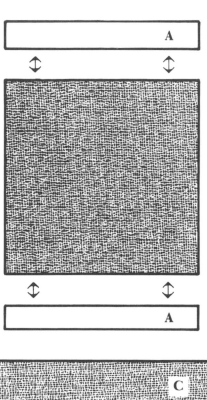

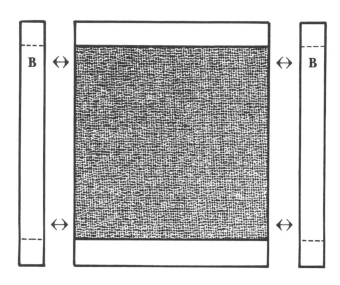

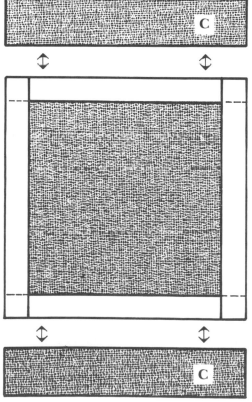

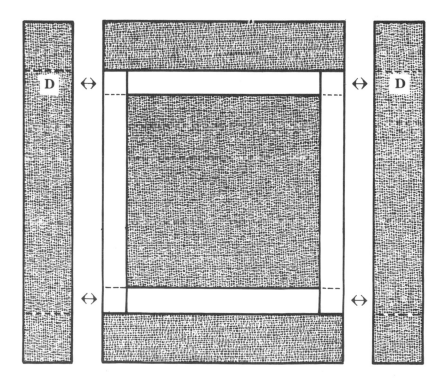

Center Diamond
Approximate size 96 x 96

Variation 1

Measurements given <u>without</u> seam allowance

A — 24½ inches square
B — 24½ inches by 6½ inches
C — 6½ inches square
D —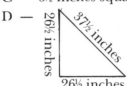

E — 53 inches by 6½ inches
F — 6½ inches square
G — 15 inches by 66 inches
H — 15 inches square

Assembly instructions:

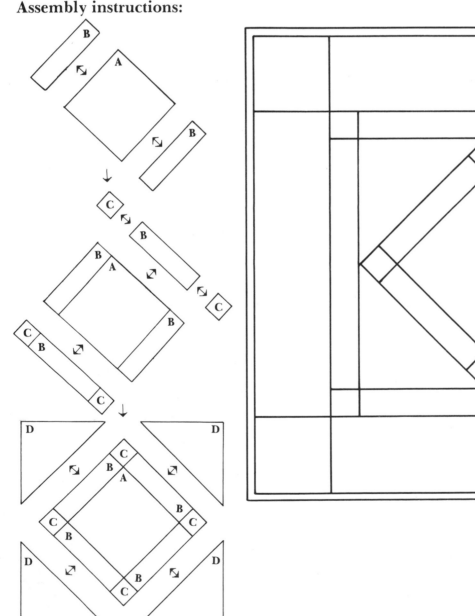

See Border Application Diagram, pg. 17.

Variation 2

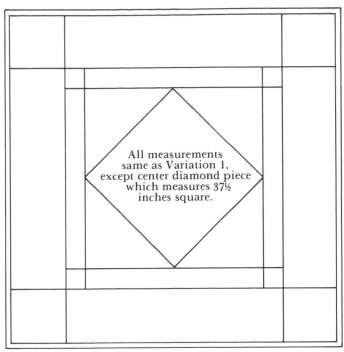

All measurements same as Variation 1, except center diamond piece which measures 37½ inches square.

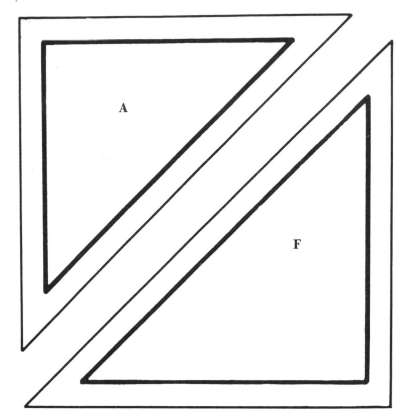

A

F

Variation 3 — Sawtooth Diamond

Measurements given <u>without</u> seam allowance

A — triangle template given
B — 13 1/16 inches square
C — 18¼ inches by 5¼ inches
D — 28¾ inches by 5¼ inches
E —

24 inches
33 15/16 inches
24 inches

F — triangle template given
G — 54 inches by 6 inches
H — 66 inches by 6 inches
I — 72 inches by 12 inches
J — 96 inches by 12 inches

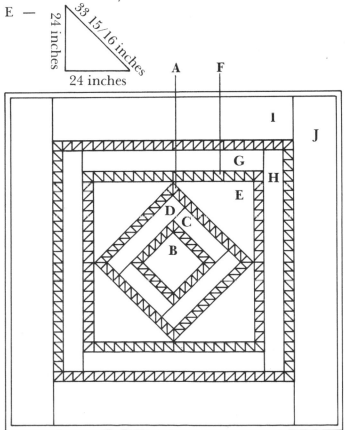

Assembly instructions:

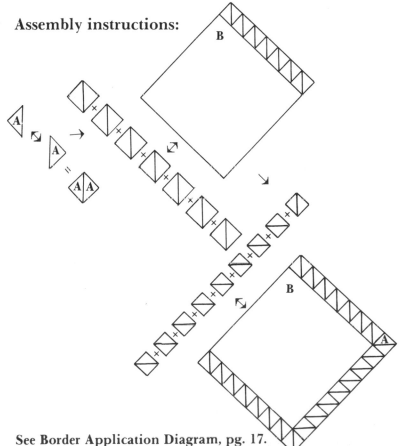

See Border Application Diagram, pg. 17.

Sunshine and Shadow
Approximate size 96 x 96

Variation 1

Measurements given <u>without</u> seam allowance

A — square template given
B — 53% inches by 6 3/16 inches
C — 66 inches by 6 3/16 inches
D — 66 inches by 15 inches
E — 15 inches square

Assembly instructions:

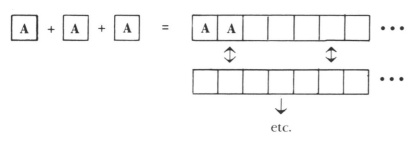

etc.

See Border Application Diagram, pg. 17.

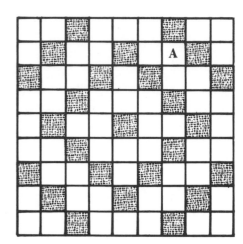

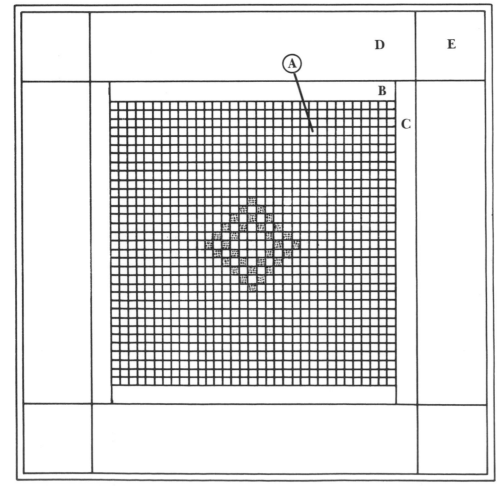

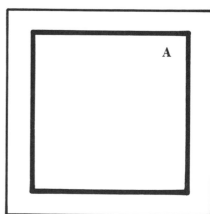

Variation 2 — Center Diamond

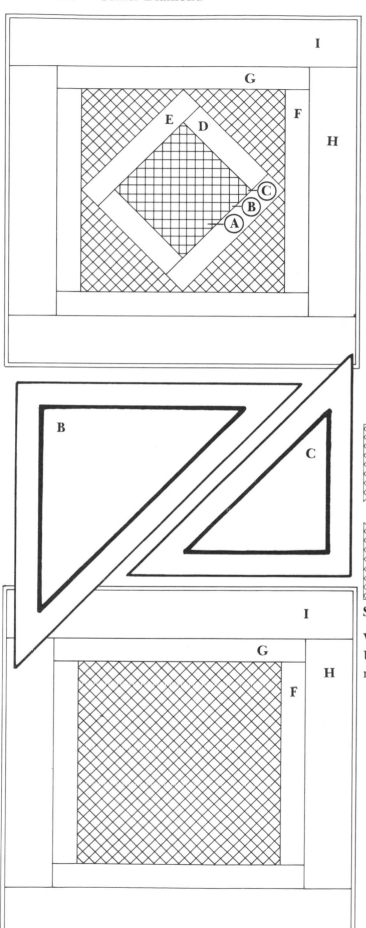

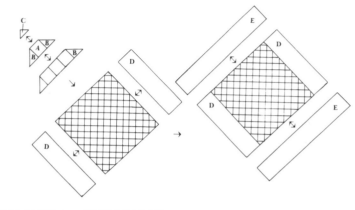

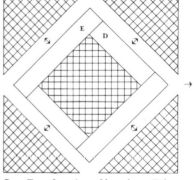

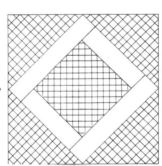

Measurements given <u>without</u> seam allowance

A — square template given
B — triangle template given
C — triangle template given
D — 24 inches by 6 inches
E — 36 inches by 6 inches
F — 51 inches by 6 inches
G — 63 inches by 6 inches
H — 63 inches by 16 inches
I — 95 inches by 16 inches

Assembly instructions:

See Border Application Diagram, pg. 17.

Variation 3
Use templates A, B, and C and other indicated
measurements from variation 2.

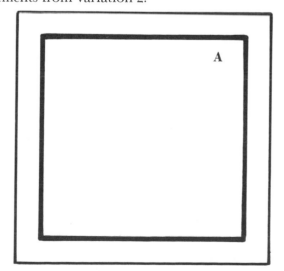

Bars
Approximate size 97 x 97

Variation 1

Measurements given <u>without</u> seam allowance
A — 8½ inches by 57¾ inches
B — 4¾ inches by 57¾ inches
C — 4¾ inches square
D — 15 inches by 67¼ inches
E — 15 inches square

Variation 2

Measurements given <u>without</u> seam allowance
A — 9½ inches by 66½ inches
B — 15 inches by 66½ inches
C — 15 inches square

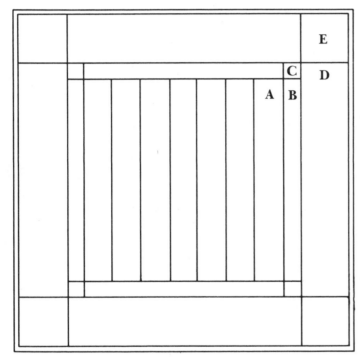

Assembly instructions:

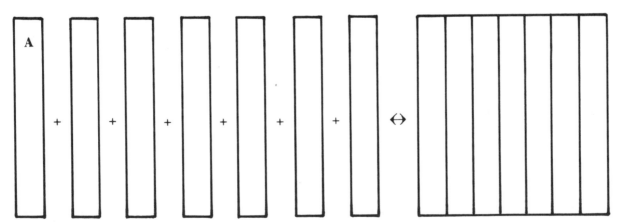

See Border Application Diagram, pg. 17.

Wild Goose Chase Variation

Measurements given <u>without</u> seam allowance

A — triangle template given
B — triangle template given
C — 9 inches by 90 inches
D — 3 inches by 72 inches
E — 3 inches by 96 inches
F — 8 inches by 78 inches
G — 8 inches by 112 inches

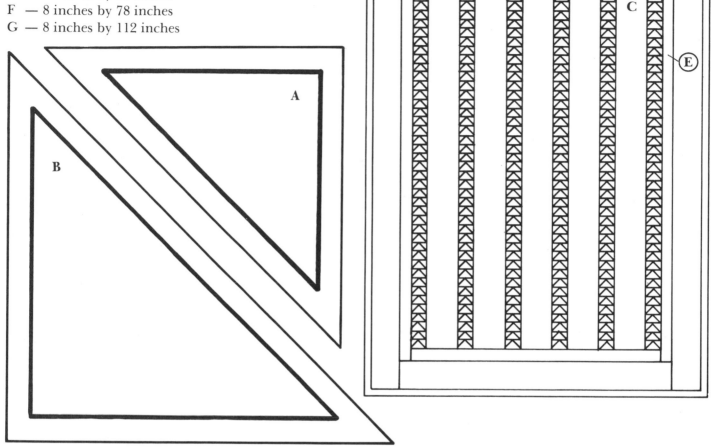

Assembly instructions:

See Border Application Diagram, pg. 17.

23

Multiple Patch
Approximate size 96 x 118

Variation 1 — Double 9-Patch

Measurements given <u>without</u> seam allowance

A — template given
B — template given
C — cut 6 squares 15¾ inches by 15¾
D — cut 10 triangles

15¾ inches / 15¾ inches

E — cut 4 triangles

12½ inches / 12½ inches

F — width of inner border 2⅝ inches
G — width of outer border 12 inches

Make 12 pieced blocks

Assembly instructions:

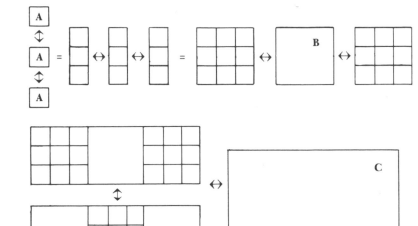

See Diagram 6, pg. 16 (Total Quilt Assembly).
See Border Application Diagram, pg. 17.

Double 4-Patch
Approximate size 96 x 104

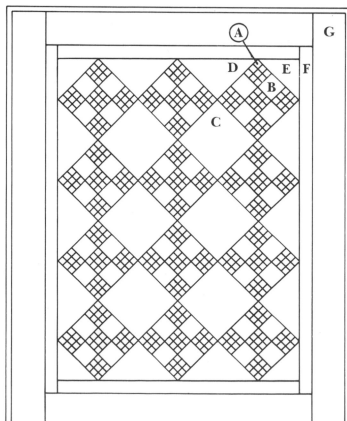

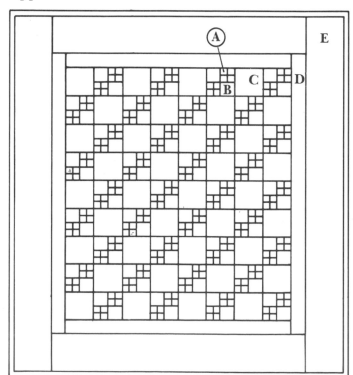

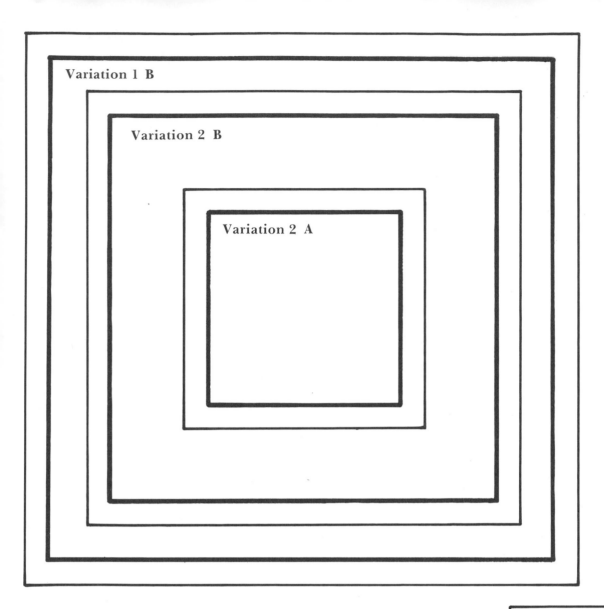

Variation 1 B

Variation 2 B

Variation 2 A

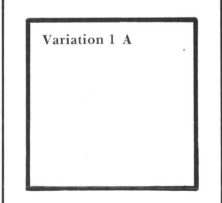

Variation 1 A

Variation 2 — Double 4-Patch

Measurements given <u>without</u> seam allowance

A — template given

B — template given

C — cut 36 squares 8 inches square

D — width of inner border — 3 inches

E — width of outer border — 13 inches

Make 20 pieced blocks

Assembly instructions:

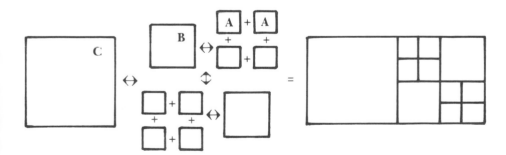

See Border Application Diagram, pg. 17.

Irish Chain
Approximate size 95 x 105

Measurements given <u>without</u> seam allowance

A — template given
B — cut 20 squares 8¾ x 8¾
C — cut 18 triangles

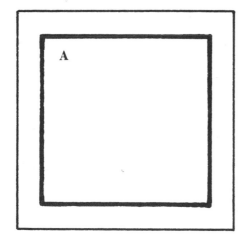

8¾ inches

8¾ inches

D — cut 4 triangles

6 3/16 inches

6 3/16 inches

E — width of inner border 3½ inches
F — width of outer border 12 inches

Make 30 pieced blocks
Plain blocks and triangles need template A and partial template A appliqued in the corners to complete the pattern.

A

Variation 1 — Double Irish Chain

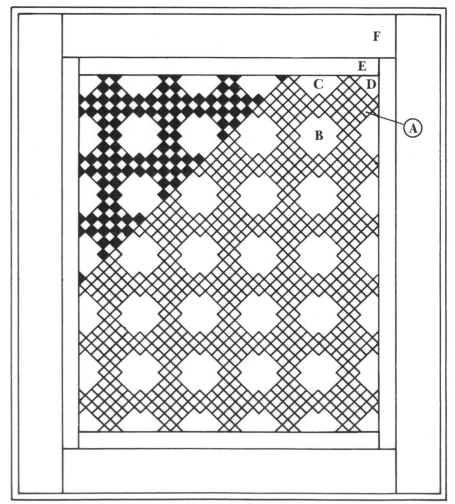

Assembly instructions:

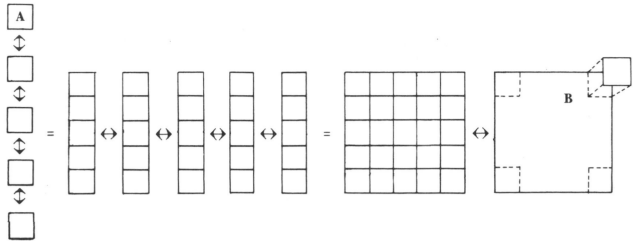

See Diagram 6, pg. 16 (Total Quilt Assembly).
See Border Application Diagram, pg. 17.

Variation 2 — Single Irish Chain
Proceed as in Variation 1 but eliminate appliqued
squares on plain alternate blocks.

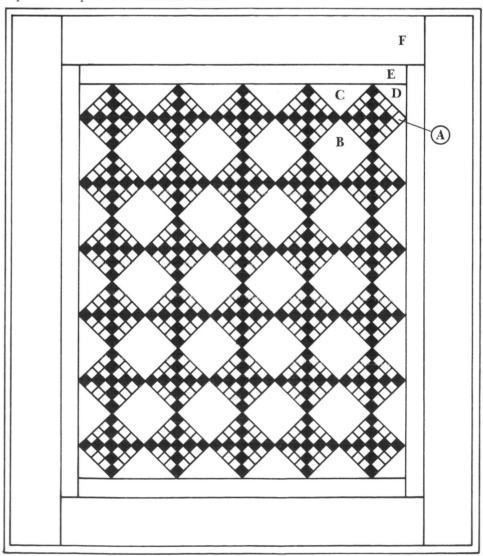

27

Log Cabin

Approximate size 96 x 108

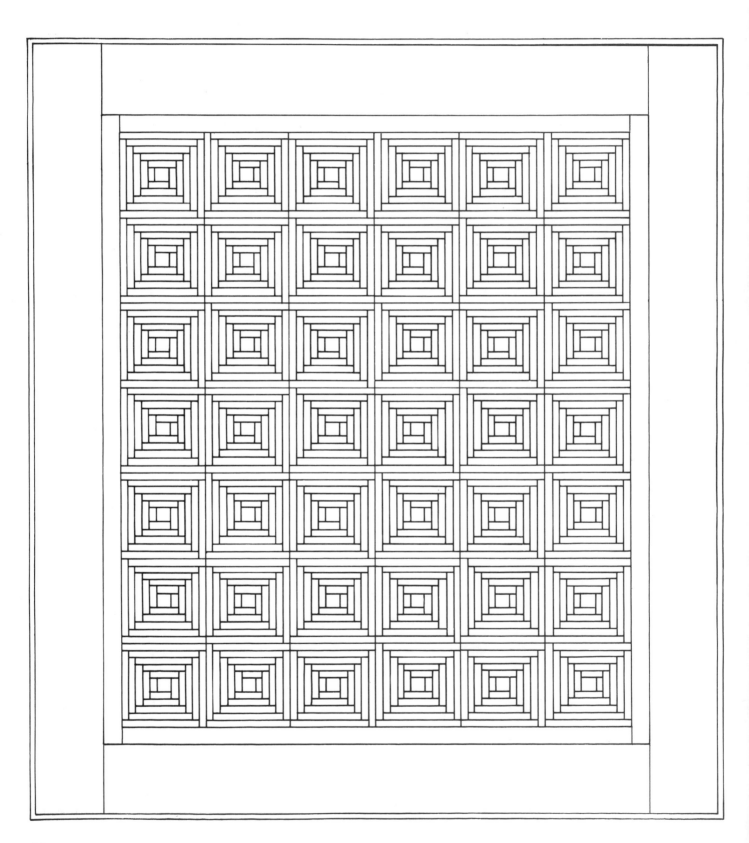

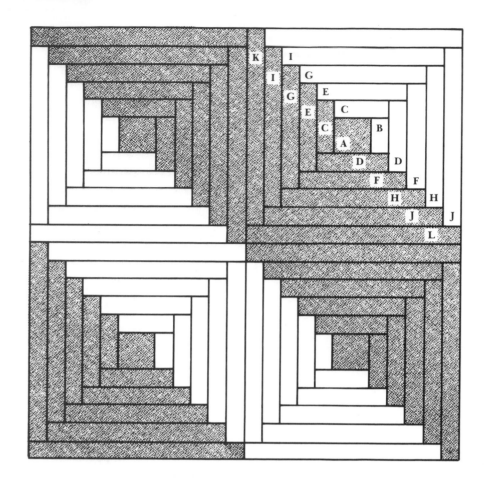

Assembly instructions:

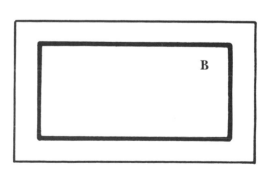

See Border Application Diagram, pg. 17.
width of inner border 3 inches
width of outer border 9 inches

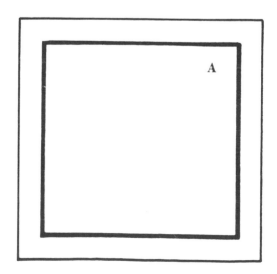

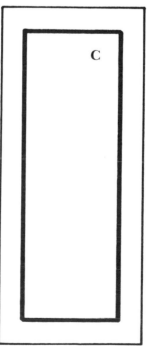

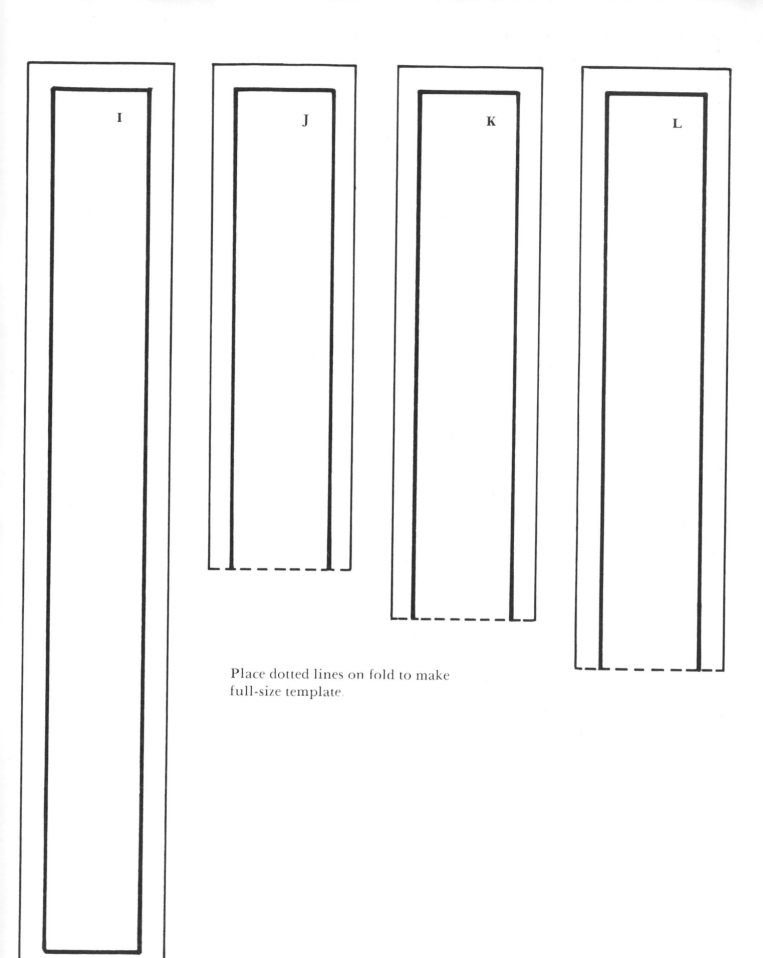

Place dotted lines on fold to make full-size template.

Double T
Approximate size 96 x 111

Measurements given <u>without</u> seam allowance

A — template given
B — template given
C — template given
D — cut 20 squares 10½ x 10½ inches
E — cut 18 triangles

10½ inches / 10½ inches

F — cut 4 triangles

7½ inches / 7½ inches

G — width of inner border 2 inches
H — width of outer border 9 inches
Make 30 pieced blocks

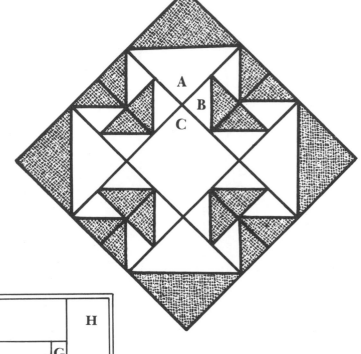

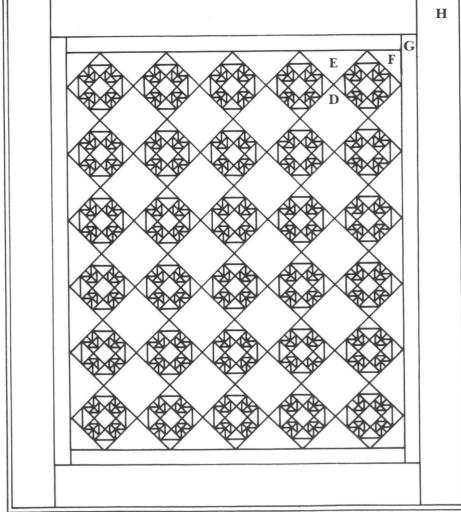

Assembly instructions:

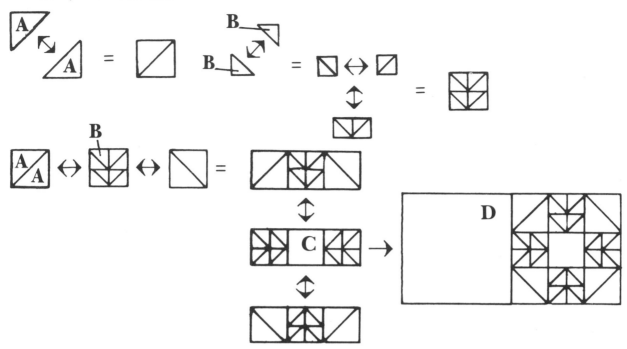

See Diagram 6, pg. 16 (Total Quilt Assembly).
See Border Application Diagram, pg. 17.

Stars

Approximate size 94 x 105

Variation 1 — Lone Star

Measurements given <u>without</u> seam allowance

A — template given

B — cut 4 squares 18 inches by 18 inches

C — cut 4 triangles

18 inches
18 inches

D — cut 9 triangles

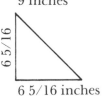

9 inches
9 inches

E — cut 2 triangles

6 5/16
6 5/16 inches

F — width of border 16 inches

Assembly instructions:

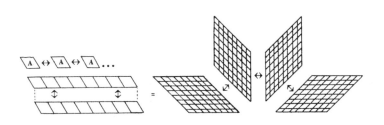

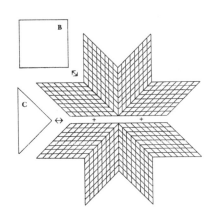

See Border Application Diagram, pg. 17.

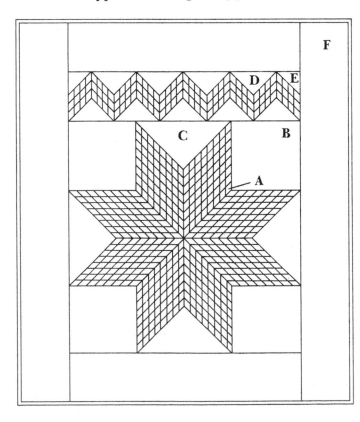

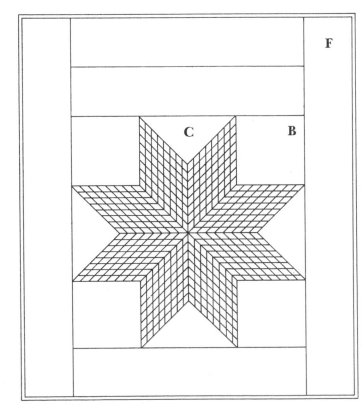

Variation 2 — Broken Star

Measurements given <u>without</u> seam allowance

A — template given (smaller than Variation 1)
B — cut 20 squares 9 inches by 9 inches
C — cut 8 triangles

D — cut 1 rectangle 12 inches by 61½ inches
E — width of border 16 inches

Assembly instructions:

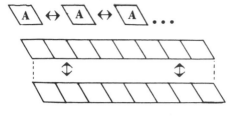

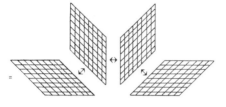

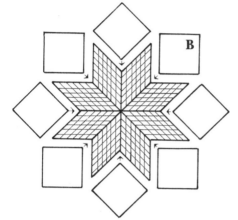

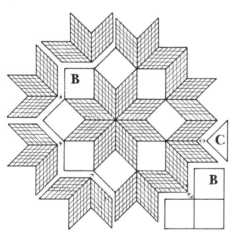

See Border Application Diagram, pg. 17.

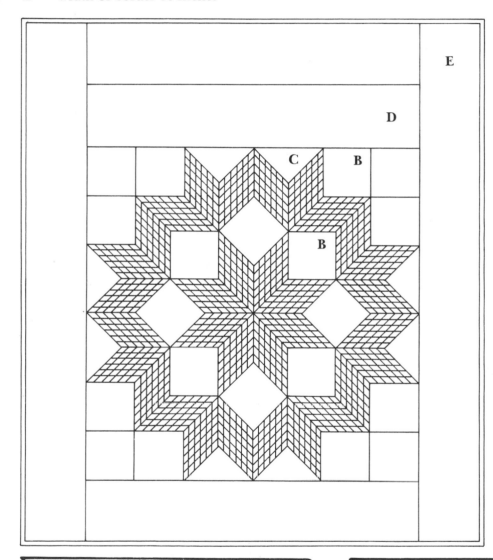

Jacob's Ladder
Approximate size 93 x 104

Measurements given <u>without</u> seam allowance

A — template given

B — template given

C — width of inner border 4 inches

D — width of outer border 11 inches

Make 42 pieced blocks

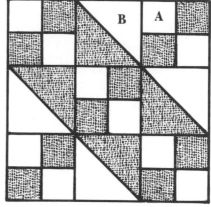

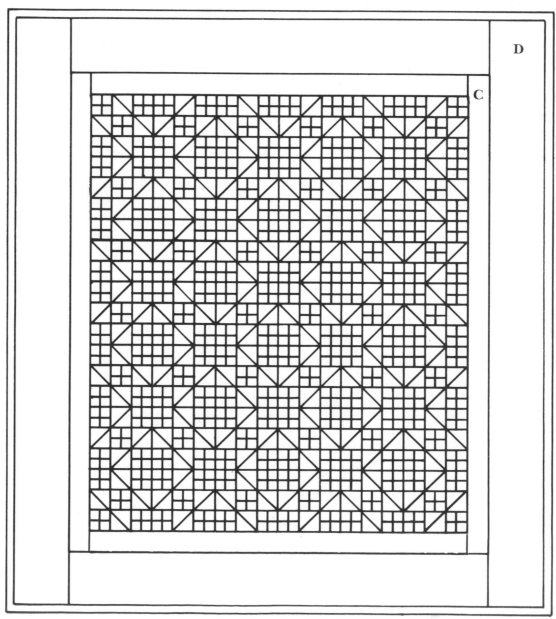

Assembly instructions:

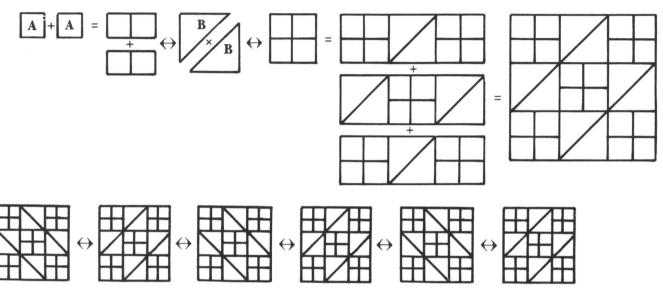

See Diagram 5, pg. 16 (Total Quilt Assembly).
See Border Application Diagram, pg. 17.

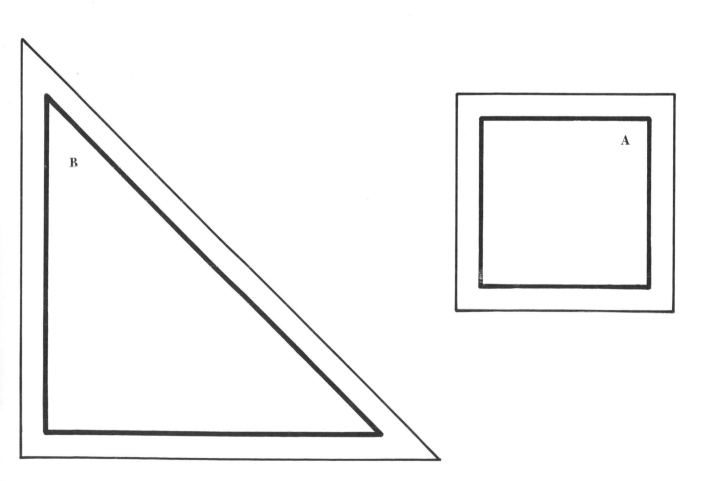

Baskets
Approximate size 90 x 105

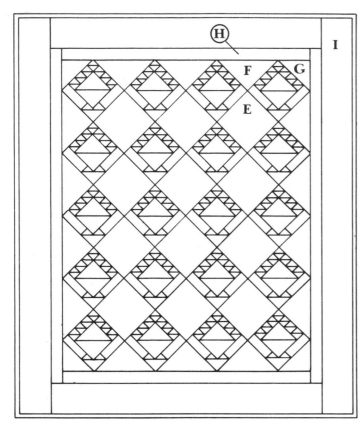

Measurements given <u>without</u> seam allowance

A — template given
B — template given
C — template given
D — template given
E — cut 12 squares 10½ by 10½ inches
F — cut 14 triangles

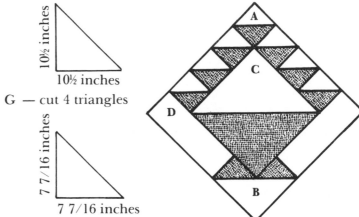

10½ inches
10½ inches

G — cut 4 triangles

7 7/16 inches
7 7/16 inches

H — width of inner border 3 inches
I — width of outer border 15 inches

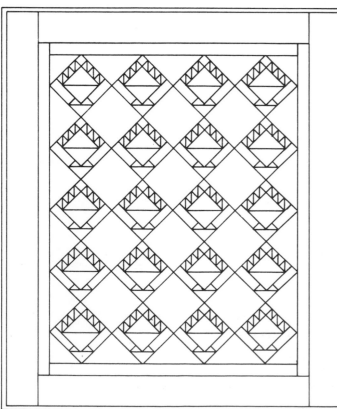

Assembly instructions:

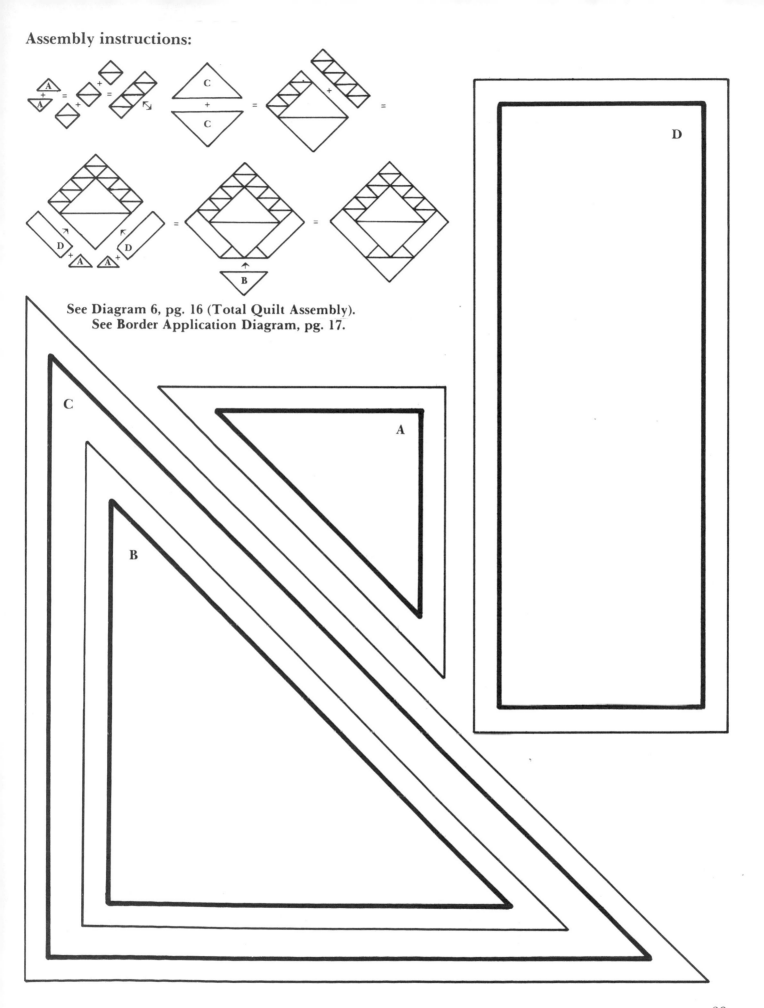

See Diagram 6, pg. 16 (Total Quilt Assembly).
See Border Application Diagram, pg. 17.

Fan
Approximate size 96 x 107

Measurements given <u>without</u> seam allowance

A — template given
B — template given
C — template given
D — width of border 15 inches

Make 42 pieced blocks

Assembly instructions:

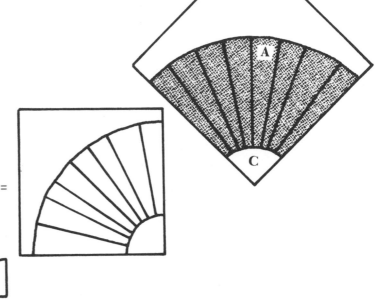

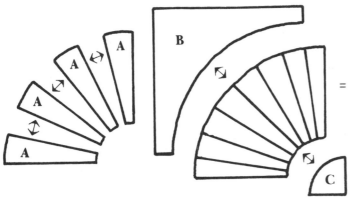

See Diagram 5, pg. 16 (Total Quilt Assembly).
See Border Application Diagram, pg. 17.

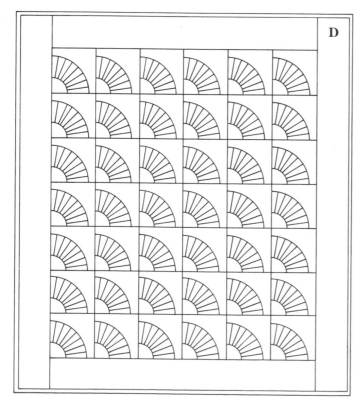

B

C

A

41

Ocean Waves
Approximate size 96 x 108

Measurements given <u>without</u> seam allowance

A — template given
B — template given
C — Cut 9 triangles

8½ inches
8½ inches

D — Cut 2 triangles

6 inches
6 inches

E — width of inner border 3 inches
F — width of outer border 9 inches

Make 15 pieced blocks
Make 11 half blocks
Make 2 quarter blocks

Darker line, below, indicates a single patch.

Assembly instructions:

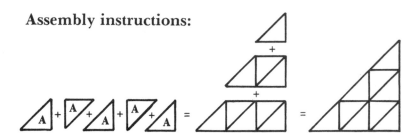

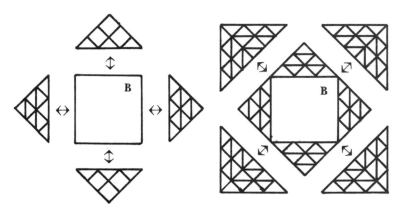

See Border Application Diagram, pg. 17.

Variation 1

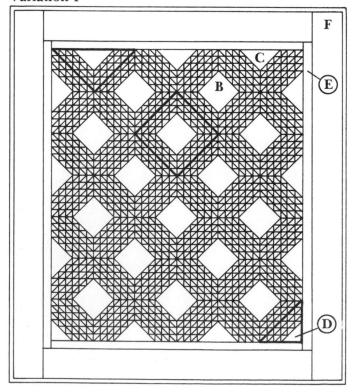

Variation 2

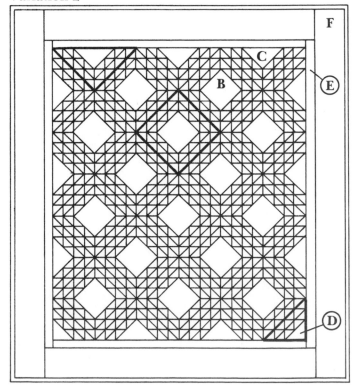

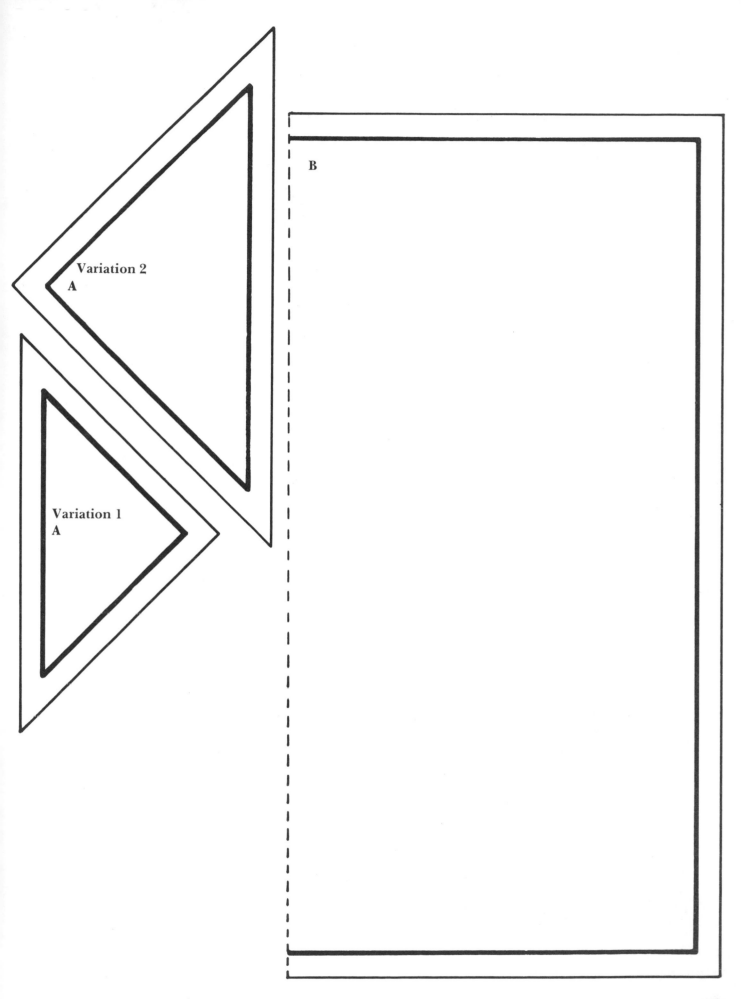

Variation 2
A

Variation 1
A

B

Roman Stripe
Approximate size 96 x 106

Measurements given <u>without</u> seam allowance

A — template given
B — template given
C — template given
D — template given
E — template given
F — cut 42 triangles

10 inches

10 inches

G — width of inner border 3 inches
H — width of outer border 15 inches

Assembly instructions:

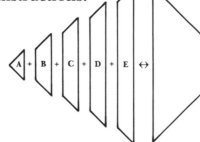

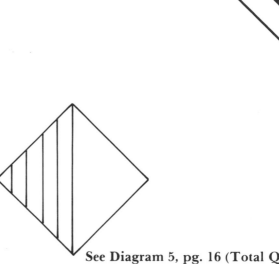

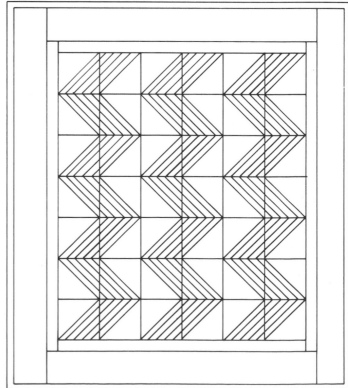

See Diagram 5, pg. 16 (Total Quilt Assembly).
See Border Application Diagram, pg. 17.

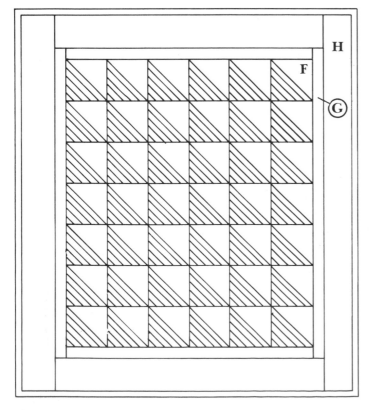

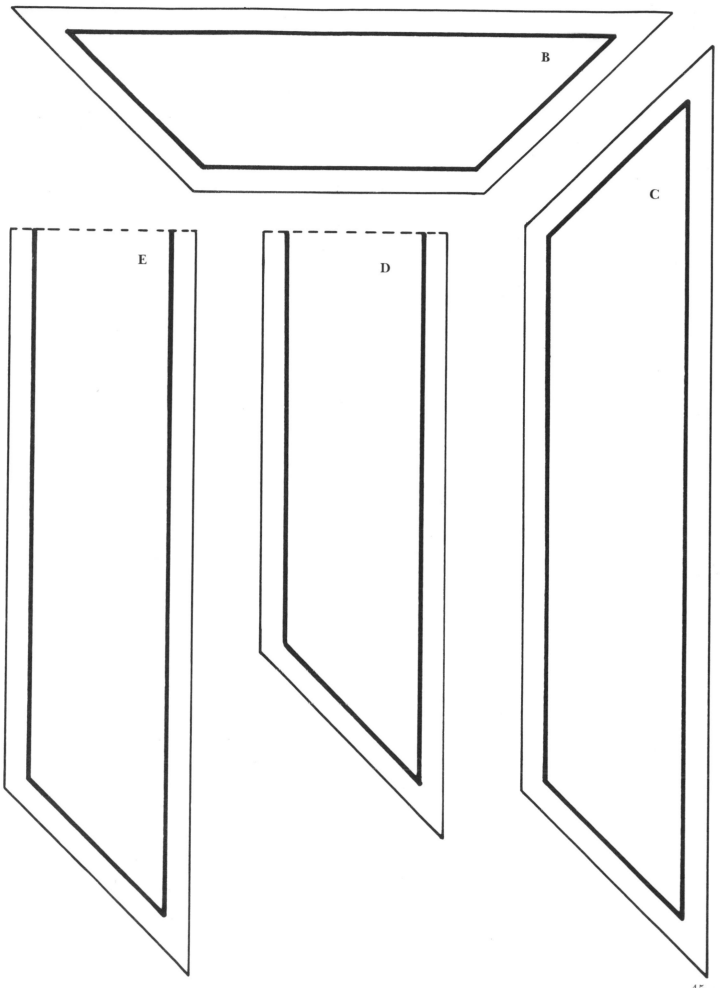

B

C

E

D

45

Tumbling Blocks
Approximate size 93 x 109

Measurements given <u>without</u> seam allowance
A — template given
B — template given
C — template given
D — width of inner border 3 inches
E — width of outer border 12 inches

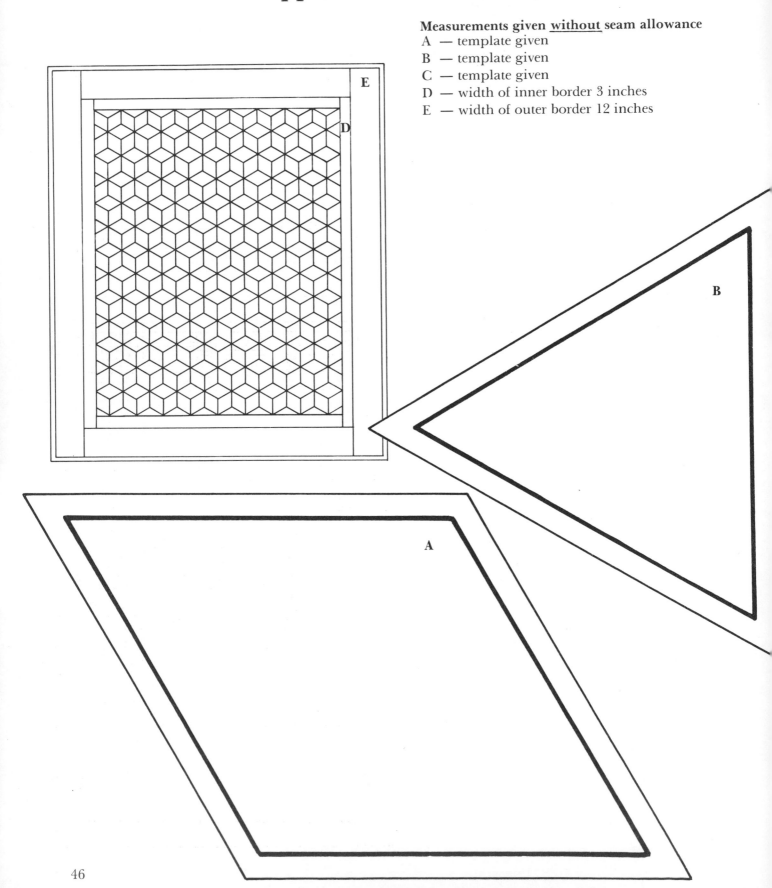

46

Assembly instructions:

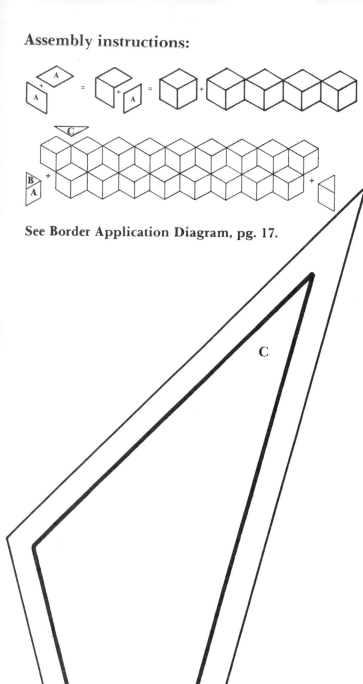

See Border Application Diagram, pg. 17.

Rail Fence
Approximate size 90 x 102

Measurements given <u>without</u> seam allowance
A — template given
B — width of inner border 3 inches
C — width of outer border 9 inches

Make 480 pieced blocks. Arrange in alternate directions to each other.

Assembly instructions:

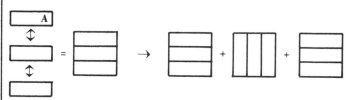

See Border Application Diagram, pg. 17.

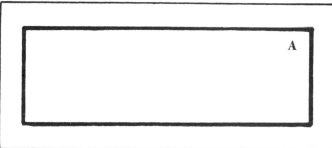

Bow Tie
Approximate size 95 x 108

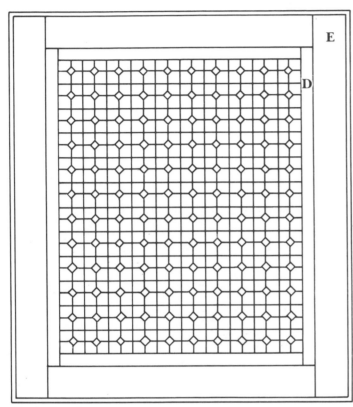

Variation 1

Measurements given <u>without</u> seam allowance

A — template given
B — template given
C — template given
D — width of inner border 3 inches
E — width of outer border 13 inches

Make 120 pieced blocks

Assembly instructions:

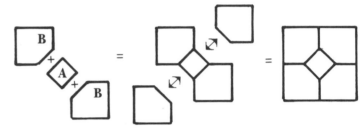

See Diagram 5, pg. 16 (Total Quilt Assembly).
See Border Application Diagram, pg. 17.

Variation 2

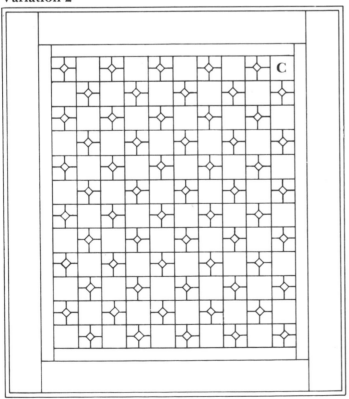

Variation 3

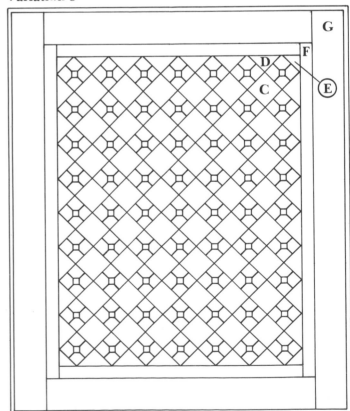

48

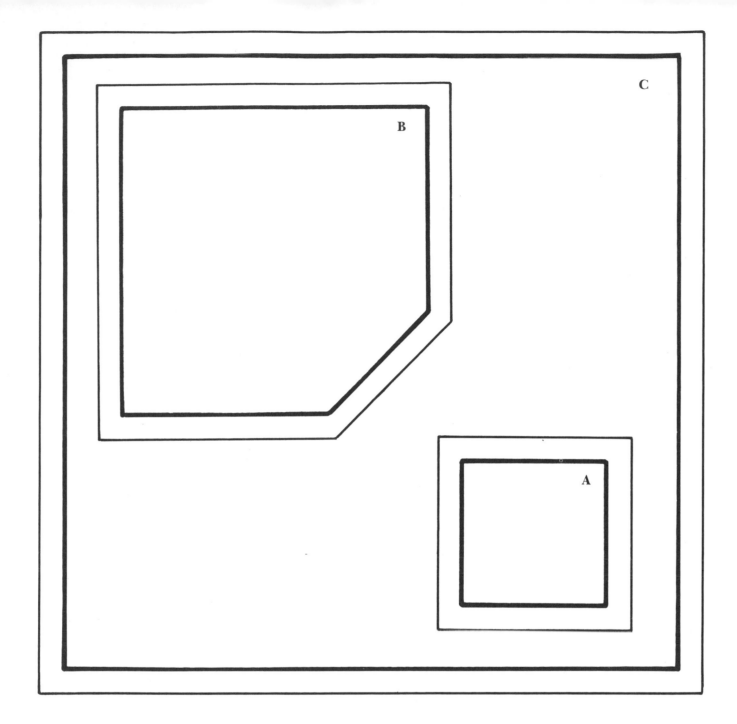

Variation 3

Mcasurcmcnts given <u>without</u> seam allowance

A — template given
B — template given
C — cut 48 squares template given
D — cut 28 triangles

E — cut 4 triangles

F — width of inner border 3 inches
G — width of outer border 13 inches

Make 63 pieced blocks

See Diagram 6, pg. 16 (Total Quilt Assembly).
See Border Application Diagram, pg. 17.

49

Robbing Peter to Pay Paul
Approximate size 96 x 106

Measurements given <u>without</u> seam allowance

A — template given
B — template given
C — width of inner border 3 inches
D — width of outer border 10 inches

Make 56 pieced blocks

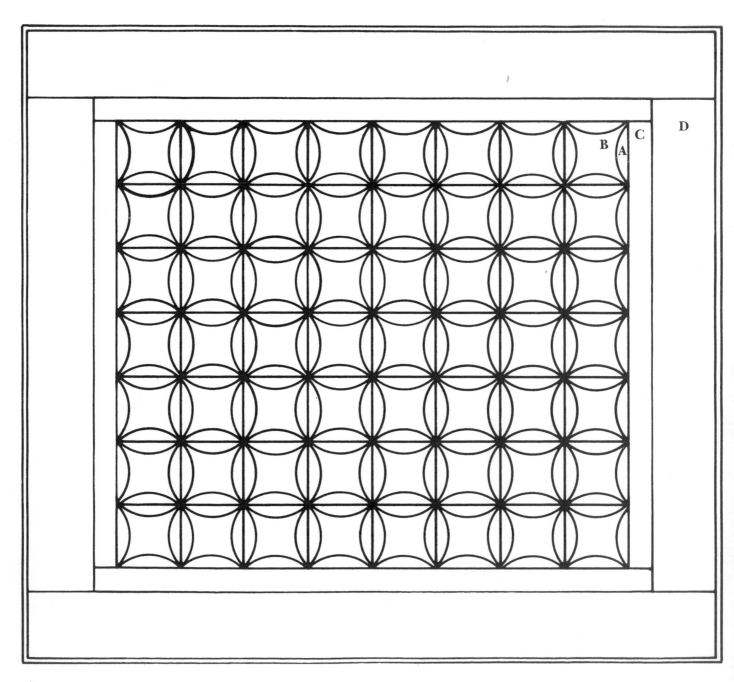

Assembly instructions:

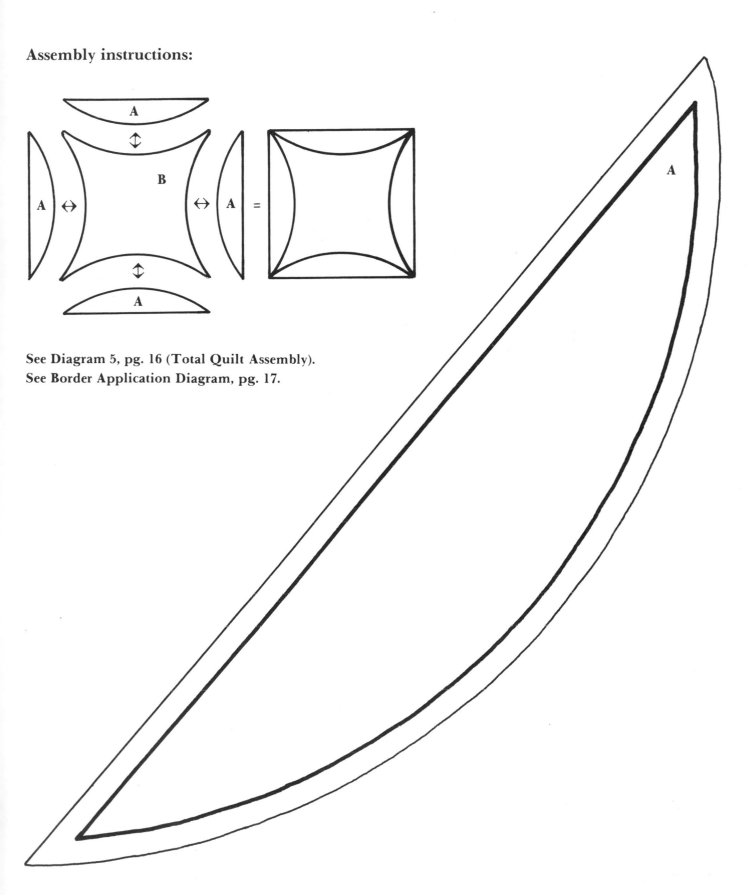

See Diagram 5, pg. 16 (Total Quilt Assembly).
See Border Application Diagram, pg. 17.

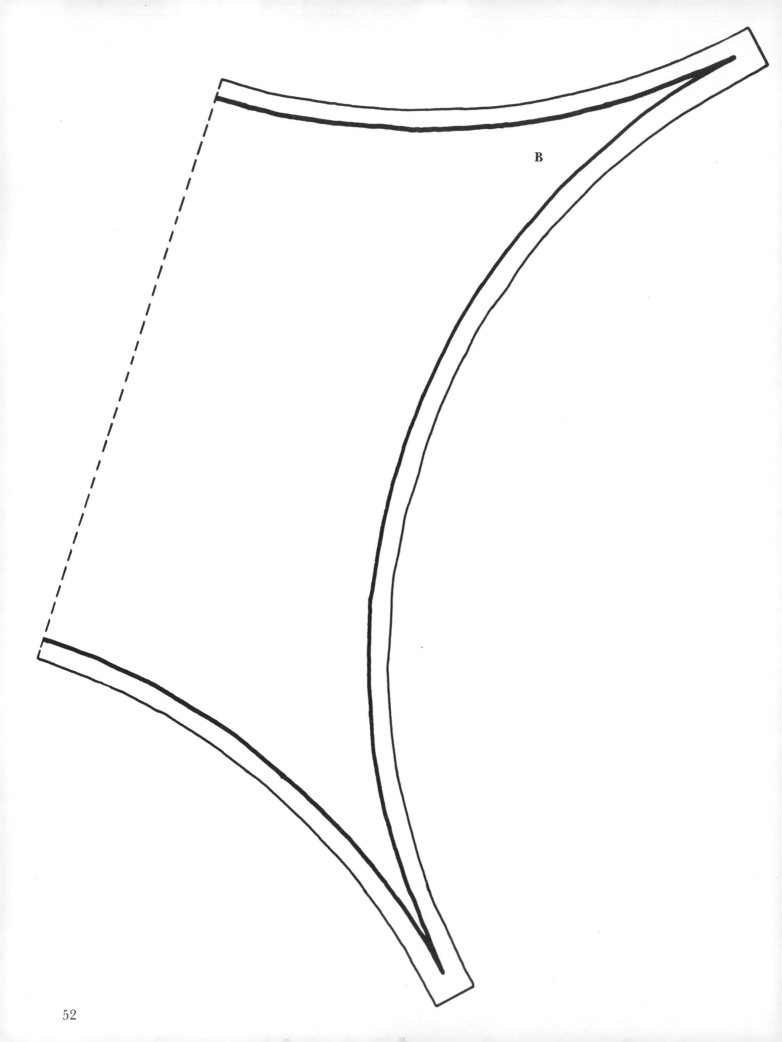

B

52

Shoo-fly
Approximate size 90 x 104

Measurements given <u>without</u> seam allowance

A — template given
B — template given
C — cut 12 squares 10½ inches by 10½ inches
D — cut 14 triangles

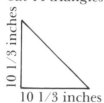

10 1/3 inches (vertical)
10 1/3 inches (horizontal)

E — cut 4 triangles

7½ inches (vertical)
7½ inches (horizontal)

F — width of inner border 3 inches
G — width of outer border 12 inches

Make 20 pieced blocks

Assembly instructions:

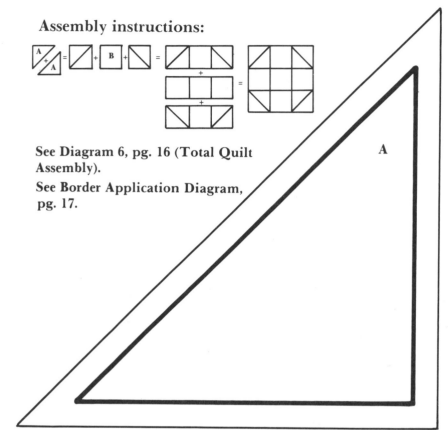

See Diagram 6, pg. 16 (Total Quilt Assembly).

See Border Application Diagram, pg. 17.

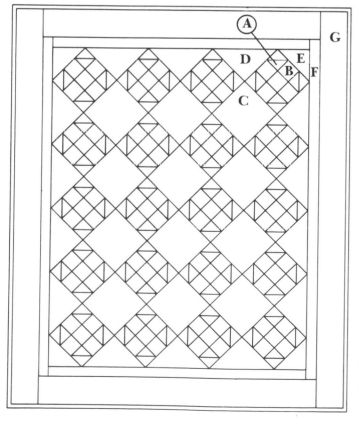

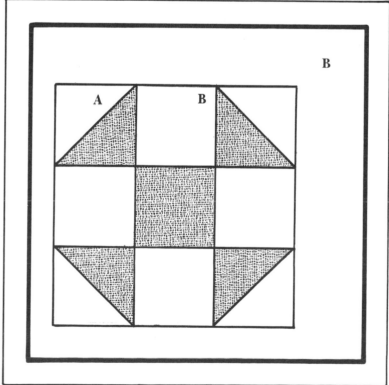

Monkey Wrench
Approximate size 88 x 102

Variation 1

Measurements given without seam allowance
A — template given
B — template given
C — width of sashing 4¼ inches
D — width of border 12 inches

Make 20 pieced blocks

Assembly instructions:

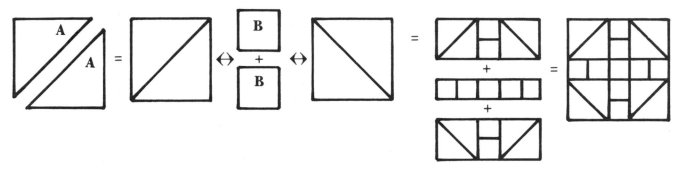

See Diagram 5, pg. 16 (Total Quilt Assembly).
See Border Application Diagram, pg. 17.

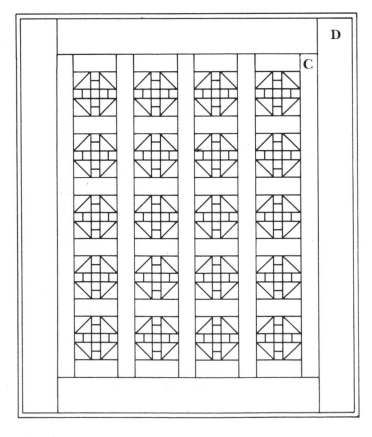

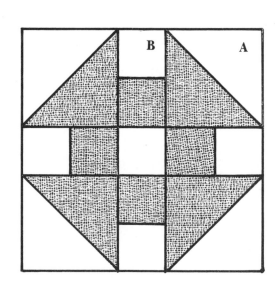

Variation 2

Measurements given <u>without</u> seam allowance

A — template given

B — template given

C — cut 12 squares 10½ inches

D — cut 14 triangles

E — cut 4 triangles

F — width of border 15 inches

Make 20 pieced blocks

See Diagram 6, pg. 16 (Total Quilt Assembly).

See Border Application Diagram, pg. 17.

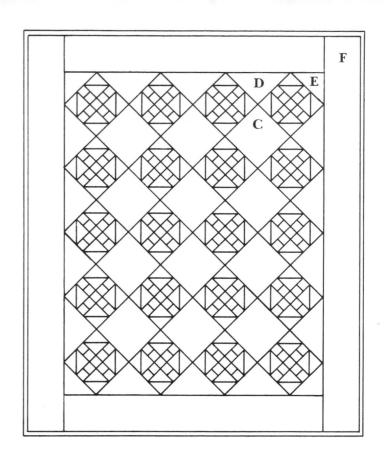

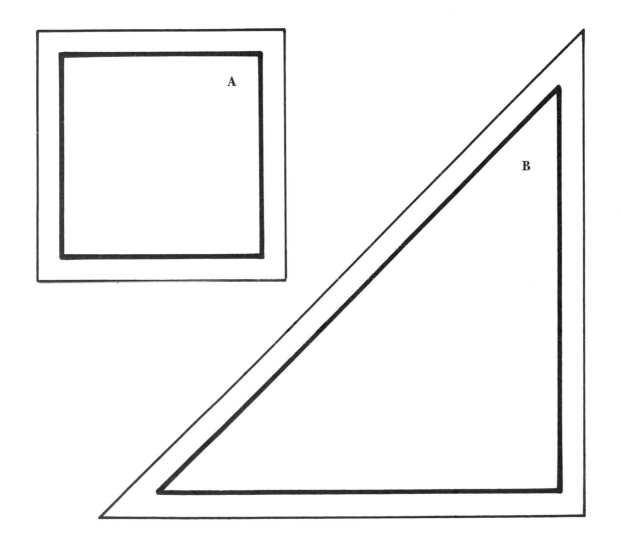

55

Carolina Lily
Approximate size 90 x 104

Measurements given <u>without</u> seam allowance

A — template given
B — template given
C — template given
D — template given
E — template given
F — template given
G — template given
H — template given
I — template given
J — template given
K — template given
L — cut 12 squares 10½ x 10½ inches

M — cut 14 triangles

10½ inches / 10½ inches

N — cut 4 triangles

7½ inches / 7½ inches

O — width of inner border 3 inches
P — width of outer border 12 inches

Make 20 pieced blocks

Assembly instructions:

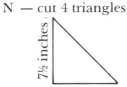

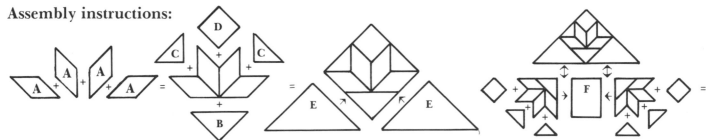

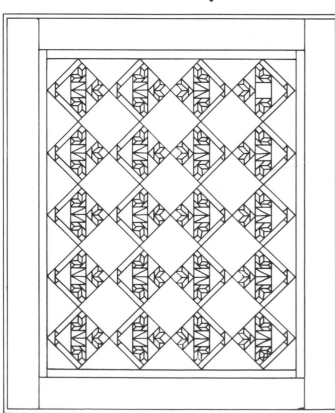

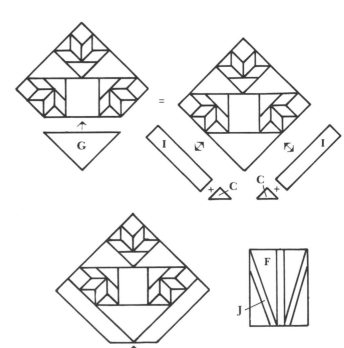

See Diagram 6, pg. 16 (Total Quilt Assembly).
See Border Application Diagram, pg. 17.

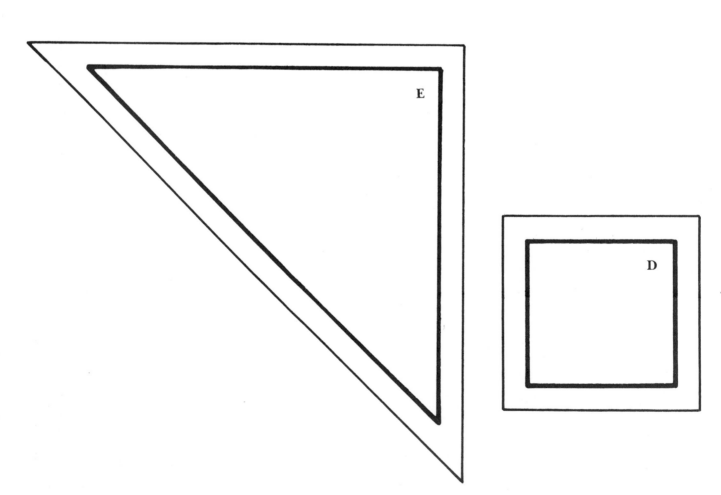

Crown of Thorns
Approximate size 90 x 104

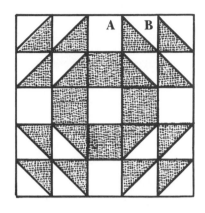

Measurements given <u>without</u> seam allowance

A — template given

B — template given

C — cut 12 squares 10½ inches by 10½ inches

D — cut 14 triangles

10½ inches / 10½ inches

E — cut 4 triangles

7½ inches / 7½ inches

F — width of inner border 3 inches

G — width of outer border 12 inches

Make 20 pieced blocks

Assembly instructions:

 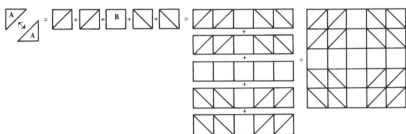

See Diagram 6, pg. 16 (Total Quilt Assembly).

See Border Application Diagram, pg. 17.

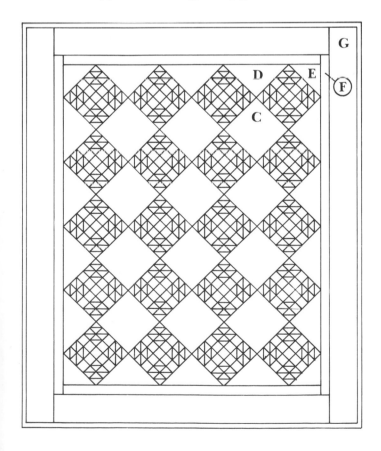

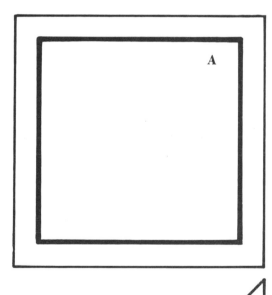

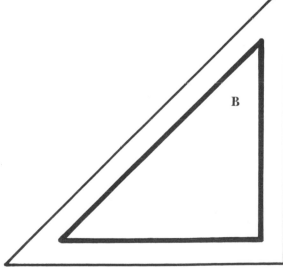

Bear Paw
Approximate size 90 x 104

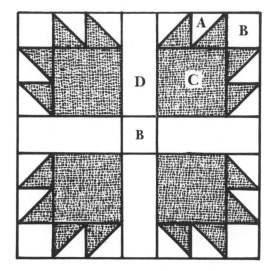

Measurements given <u>without</u> seam allowance

A — template given

B — template given

C — template given

D — template given

E — cut 12 squares 10½ x 10½ inches

F — cut 14 triangles

10½ inches / 10½ inches

G — cut 4 triangles

7½ inches / 7½ inches

H — width of inner border 3 inches

I — width of outer border 12 inches

Make 20 pieced blocks

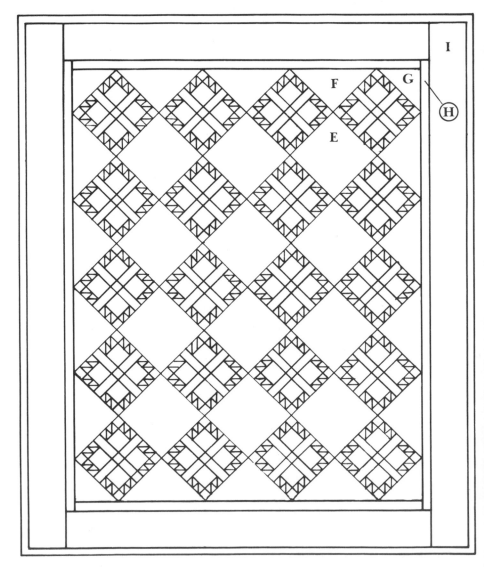

Assembly instructions:

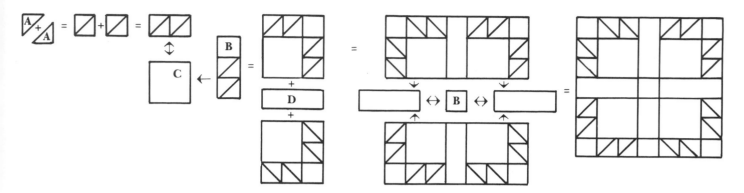

See Diagram 6, pg. 16 (Total Quilt Assembly).
See Border Application Diagram, pg. 17.

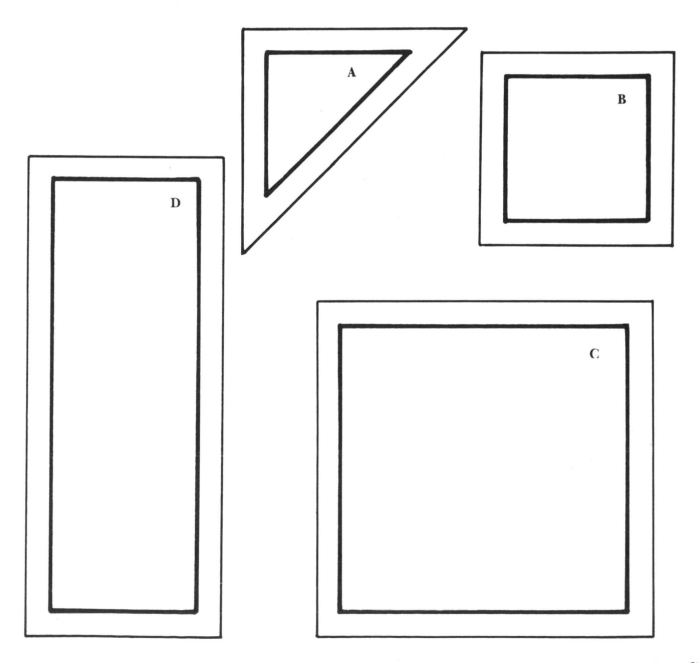

61

Pinwheel
Approximate size 90 x 104

Variation 1

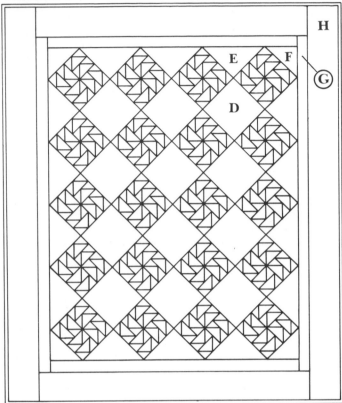

Measurements given <u>without</u> seam allowance

A — template given
B — template given
C — template given
D — cut 12 squares 10½ inches by 10½ inches
E — cut 14 triangles

F — cut 4 triangles

G — width of inner border 3 inches
H — width of outer border 12 inches

Make 20 pieced blocks

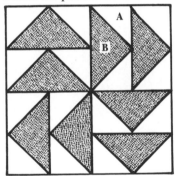 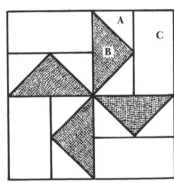

Assembly instructions:

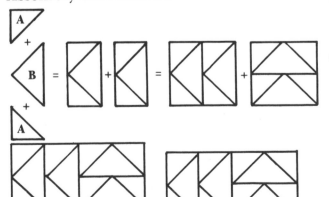

Variation 2

See Diagram 6, pg. 16 (Total Quilt Assembly).
See Border Application Diagram, pg. 17.

Variation 3

B — template given   D — template given

Use same measurements and procedures as in variation 1

Assembly instructions:

See Diagram 6, pg. 16 (Total Quilt Assembly).

See Border Application Diagram, pg. 17.

C

A

Variation 3

Variation 1, 2, 3

D

B

63

Garden Maze
Approximate size 86 x 103

Measurements given <u>without</u> seam allowance

A — template given
B — template given
C — template given
D — template given
E — template given
F — cut 12 squares 10 inches by 10 inches
G — width of inner border 3 inches
H — width of outer border 12 inches

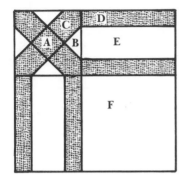

Assembly instructions:

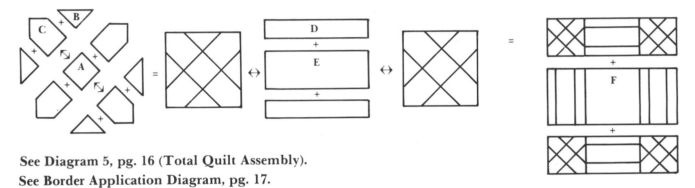

See Diagram 5, pg. 16 (Total Quilt Assembly).
See Border Application Diagram, pg. 17.

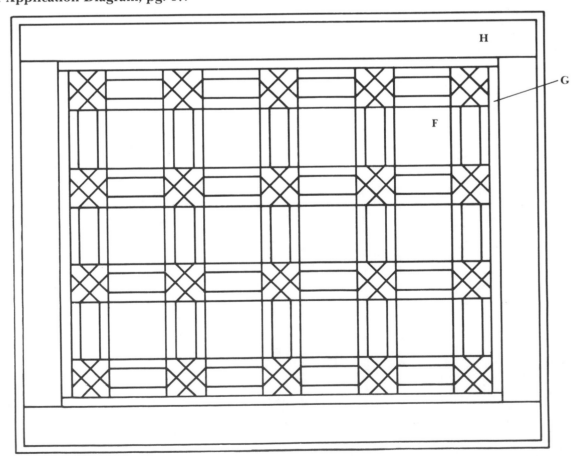

E

C

A

D

B

65

Railroad Crossing
Approximate size 92 x 112

Measurements given <u>without</u> seam allowance

A — template given
B — template given
C — cut 18 squares 10 inches by 10 inches
D — cut 10 triangles

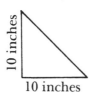

10 inches / 10 inches

E — template given
F — template given
G — width of inner border 3 inches
H — width of outer border 12 inches

Assembly instructions:

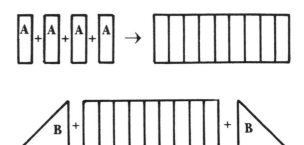

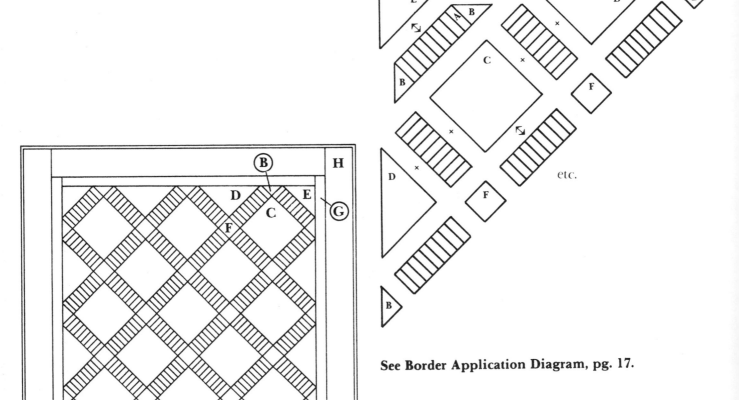

etc.

See Border Application Diagram, pg. 17.

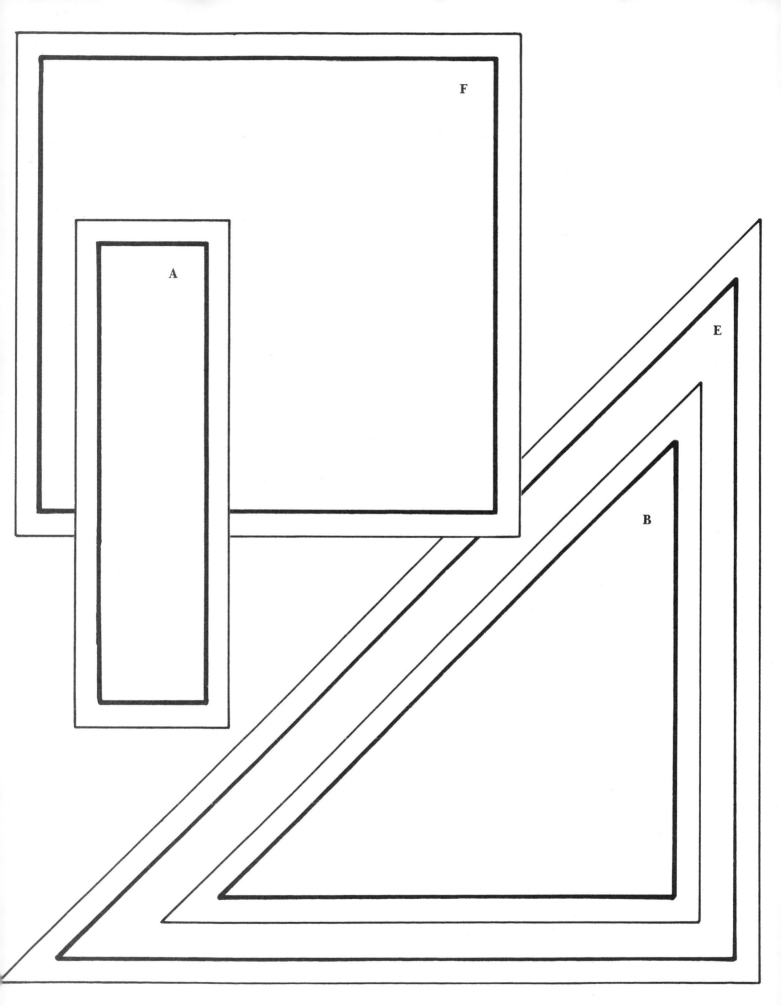

Double Wedding Ring
Approximate size 90 x 103

A — template given
B — template given
C — template given
D — template given
E — template given
F — template given

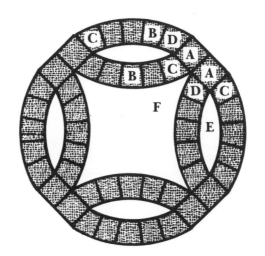

Assembly instructions:

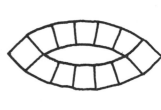

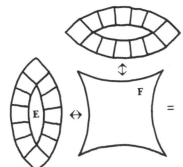

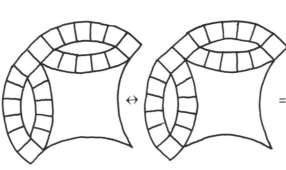

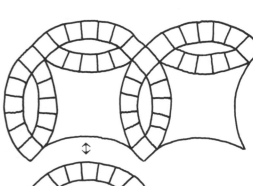

etc.

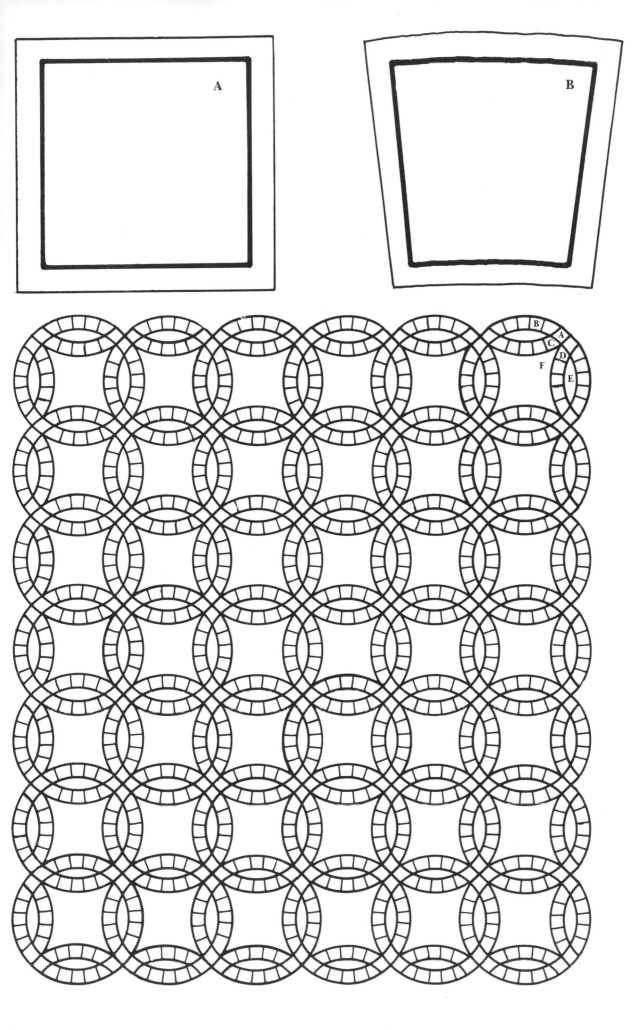

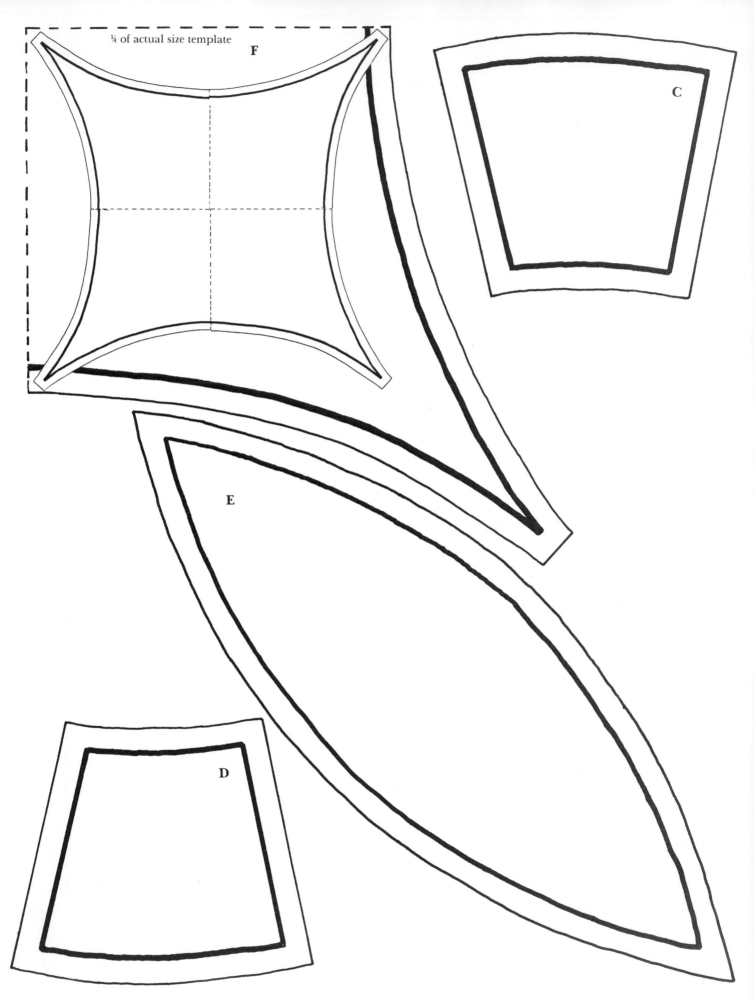

¼ of actual size template

F

C

E

D

Diagonal Triangles
Approximate size 90 x 96

Measurements given <u>without</u> seam allowance
A — template given
B — width of inner border 3 inches
C — width of outer border 12 inches

Assembly instructions:

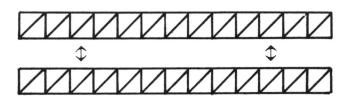

See Border Application Diagram, pg. 17.

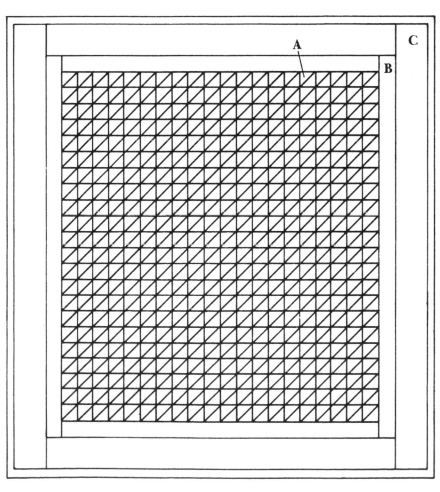

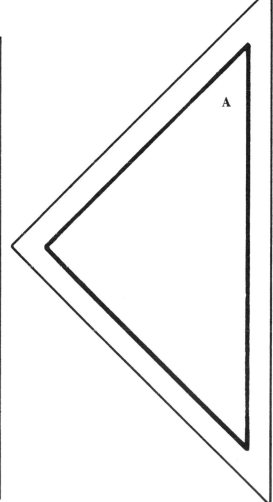

Drunkard's Path
Approximate size 102 x 128

Measurements given <u>without</u> seam allowance

A — template given
B — template given
C — width of inner border 3 inches
D — width of outer border 9 inches

Make 192 pieced blocks. Alternate placement of blocks
to match diagram.

Assembly instructions:

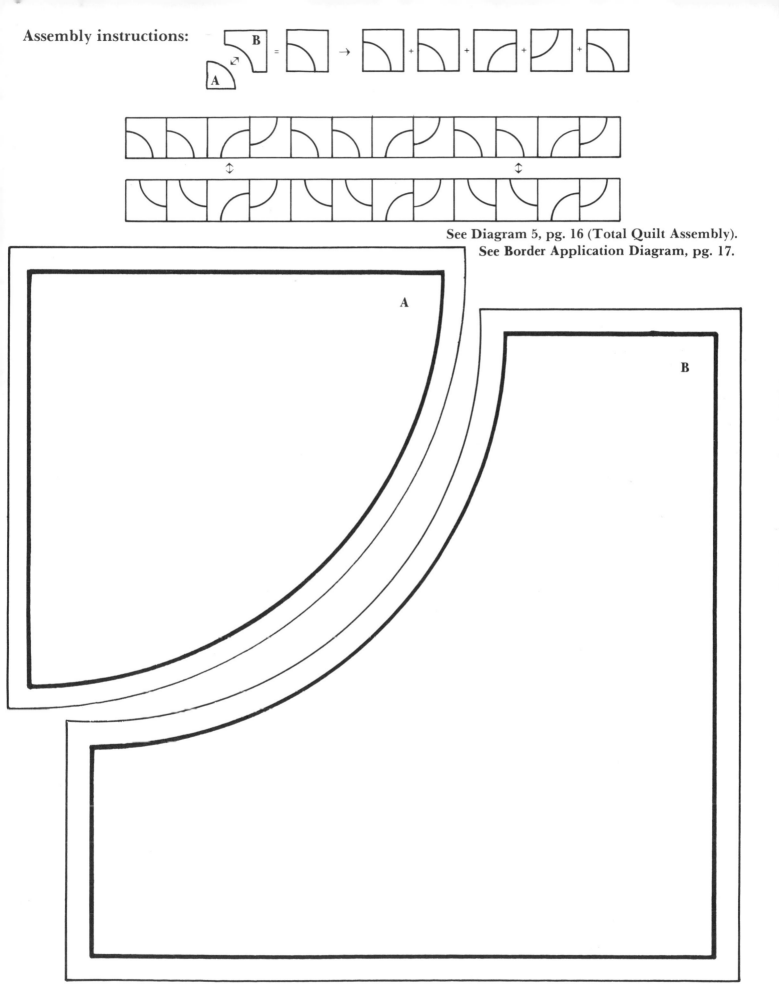

See Diagram 5, pg. 16 (Total Quilt Assembly).
See Border Application Diagram, pg. 17.

A

B

73

Tree of Life

Approximate size 94 x 114

Measurements given <u>without</u> seam allowance

A — template given
B — template given
C — template given
D — template given
E — template given
F — template given
G — cut 6 squares 15¾ x 15¾ inches
H — cut 10 triangles

I — cut 4 triangles

J — width of inner border 3 inches
K — width of outer border 12 inches

Make 12 pieced blocks

Assembly instructions:

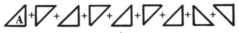

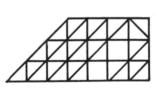

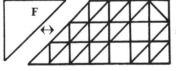 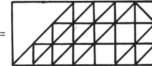 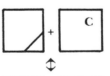 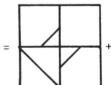 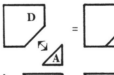 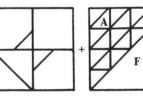

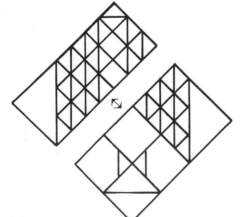 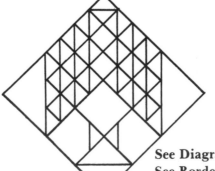

See Diagram 6, pg. 16 (Total Quilt Assembly).
See Border Application Diagram, pg. 17.

74

75

E

A

B

C

D

F

Bachelor's Puzzle
Approximate size 96 x 110

Measurements given <u>without</u> seam allowance

A — template given

B — template given

C — template given

D — width of inner border 3 inches

E — width of outer border 12 inches

Pieced blocks must be alternated as in diagram to create the proper pattern

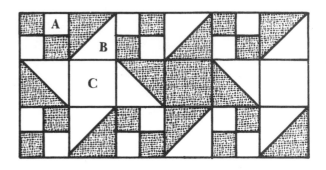

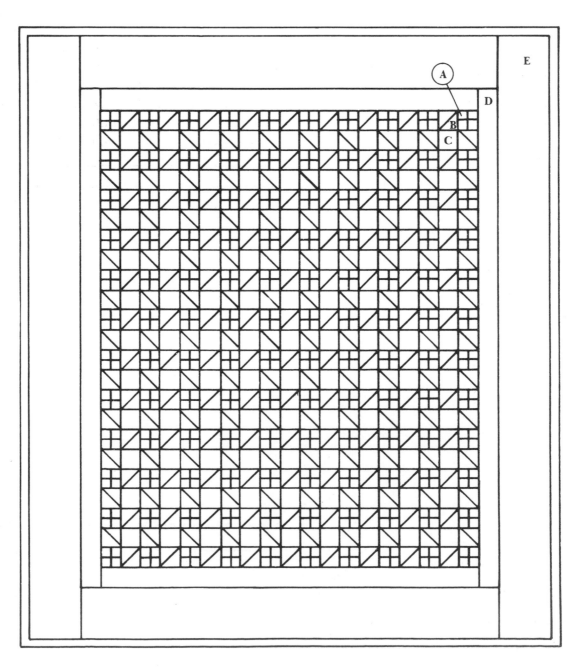

Assembly instructions:

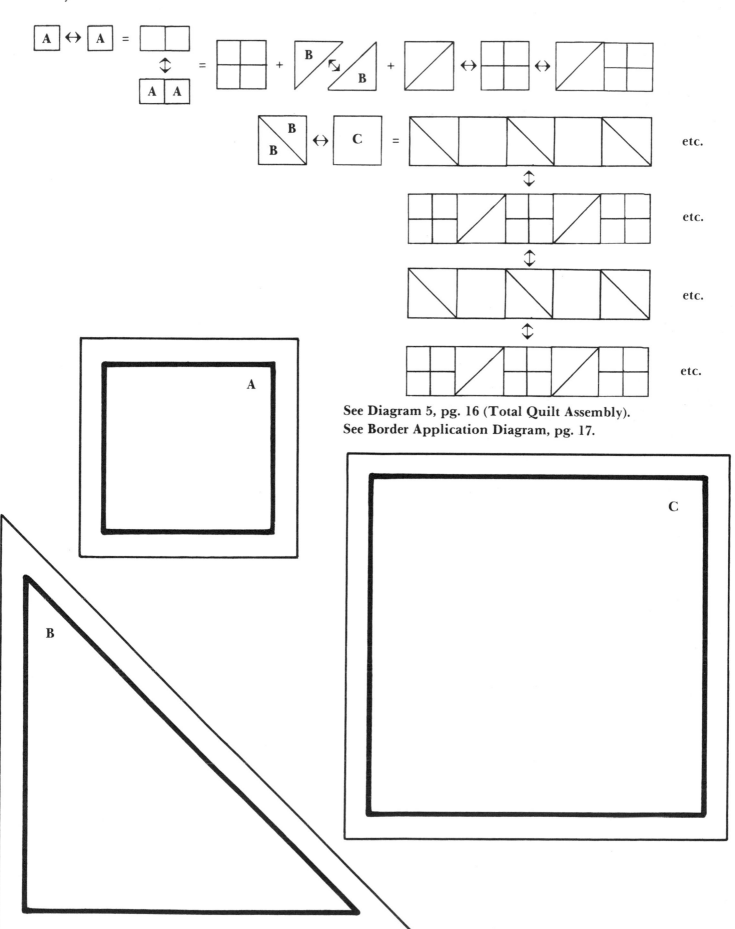

See Diagram 5, pg. 16 (Total Quilt Assembly).
See Border Application Diagram, pg. 17.

Rolling Stone

Approximate size 90 x 104

Measurements given <u>without</u> seam allowance

A — template given
B — template given
C — template given
D — cut 12 squares 10½ by 10½ inches
E — cut 14 triangles

10½ inches
10½ inches

F — cut 4 triangles

7½ inches
7½ inches

G — width of inner border 3 inches
H — width of outer border 12 inches

Make 20 pieced blocks

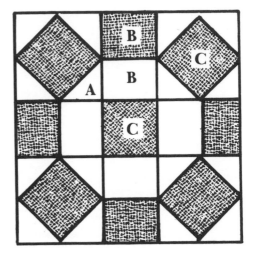

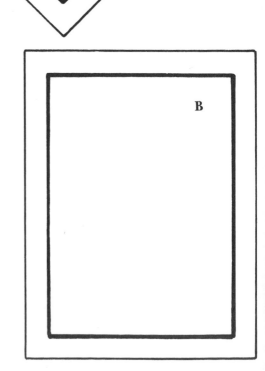

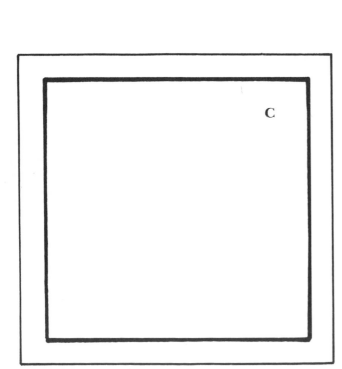

Assembly instructions:

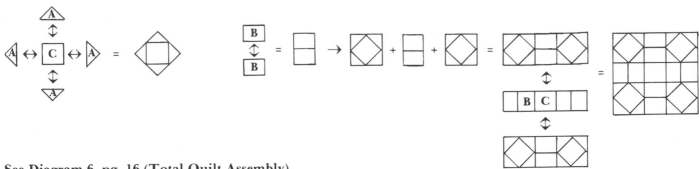

See Diagram 6, pg. 16 (Total Quilt Assembly).
See Border Application Diagram, pg. 17.

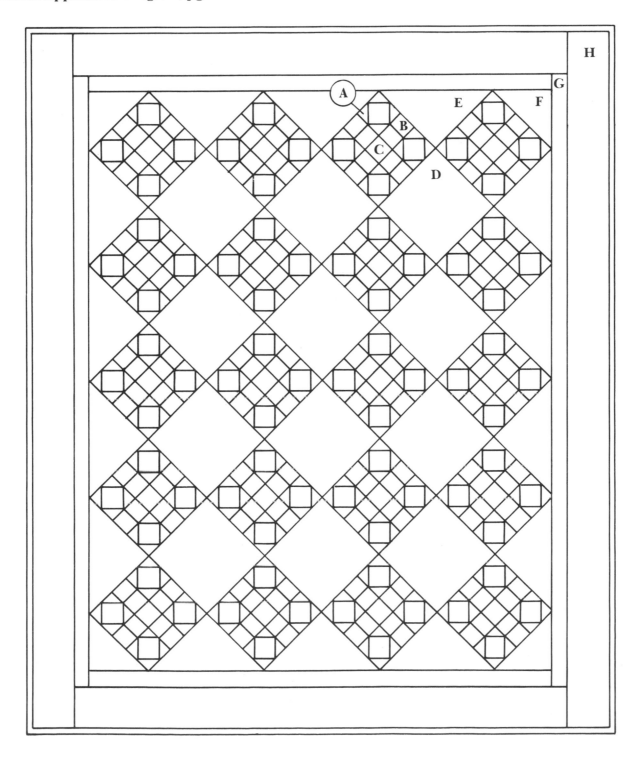

Quilting Templates

Following are several traditional quilting templates given in full size. Many of the templates extend over several pages. To use, pull out template section along perforation. Match corresponding letters along dotted lines and tape pages together to form the complete template.

One quarter of the Circular Feather is given. To make a complete circle, trace the section given, make a one-quarter turn, and trace again. Repeat until circle is complete.

Circular Feather — i.

To create finished template, match corresponding letters
along dotted lines, and tape.

Completed pattern motif will look like this:

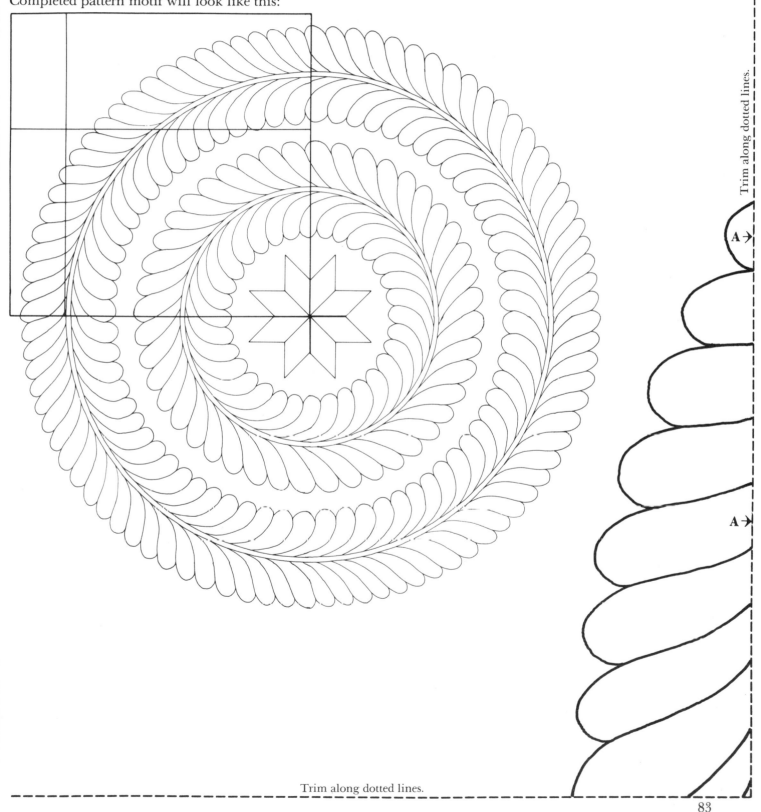

Circular Feather — ii.

Trim along dotted lines.

Trim along dotted lines.

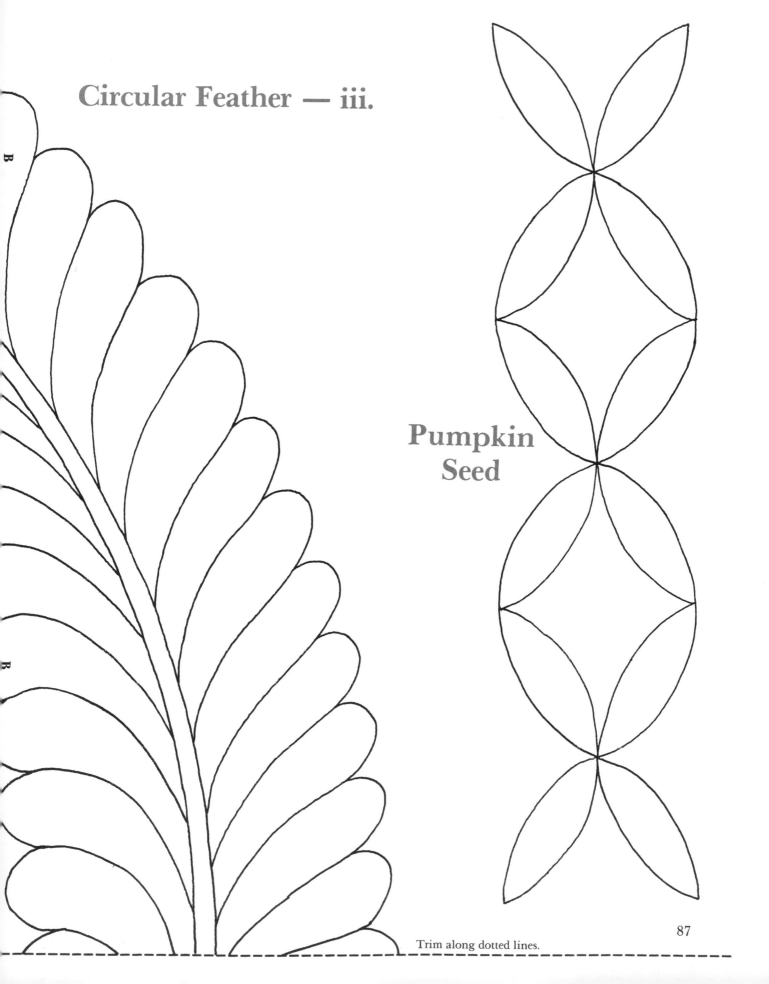

Circular Feather — iii.

B

Pumpkin Seed

B

Triangular Rose — i.

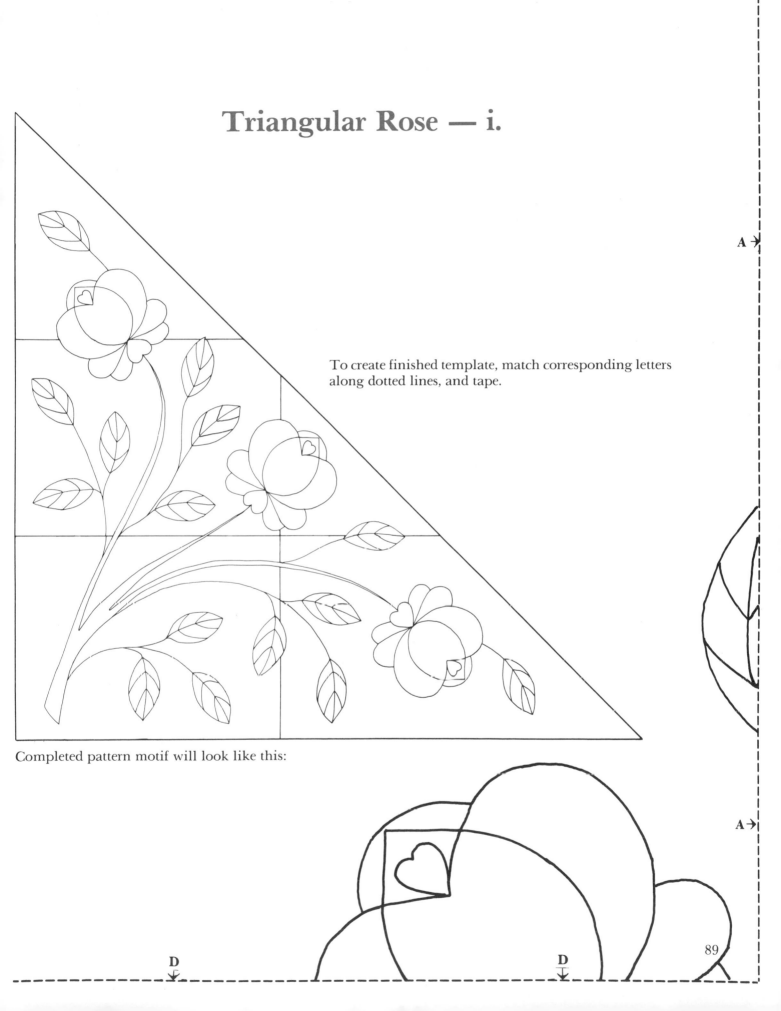

To create finished template, match corresponding letters along dotted lines, and tape.

Completed pattern motif will look like this:

A →

A →

D

D

Triangular Rose — ii.

← A

B

Trim along dotted lines.

B

C

Triangular Rose — iii.

C

D

D

← E

C →

Triangular Rose — iv.

← E

C →

Triangular Rose — v.

E →

Ivy Leaf

E →

Feather Border — i.

← A

Trim along dotted lines.

← A

Completed pattern motif will look like this:

To create finished template, match corresponding letters along dotted lines, and tape.

Feather Border — ii.

A

B →

B →

C

C

101

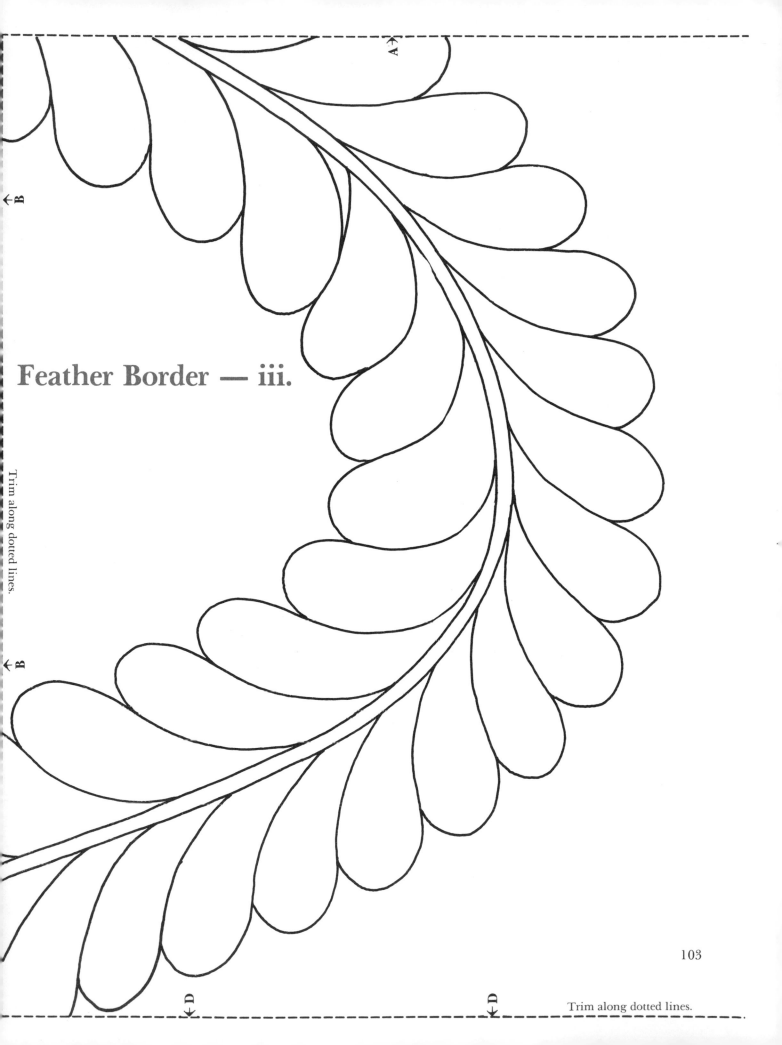

Feather Border — iii.

←B

←B

←D ←D

Trim along dotted lines.

103

Trim along dotted lines.

Feather Border — iv.

E

E

Trim along dotted lines.

C

C Trim along dotted lines.

Feather Border — v.

Grapes with Leaves

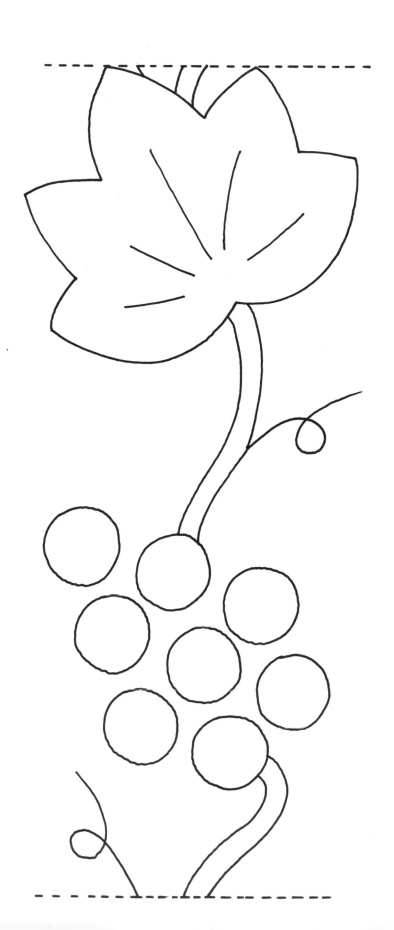

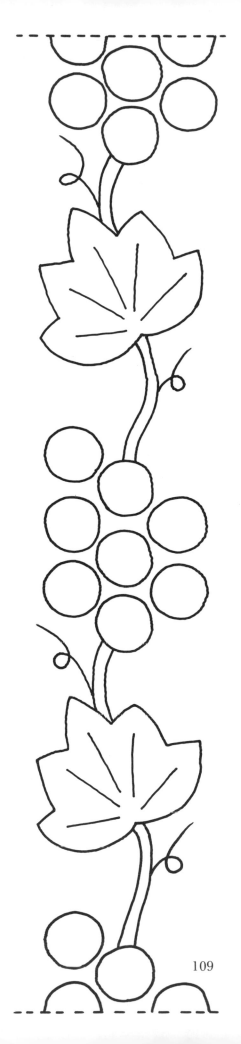

Grapes with Leaves

109

Fiddlehead Fern — i.

To create finished template, match corresponding letters
along dotted lines, and tape.

Completed pattern motif will look like this:

A →

Trim along dotted lines.

A →

D

Trim along dotted lines.

D

Fiddlehead Fern — ii.

Trim along dotted lines.

← A

B

B

Trim along dotted lines.

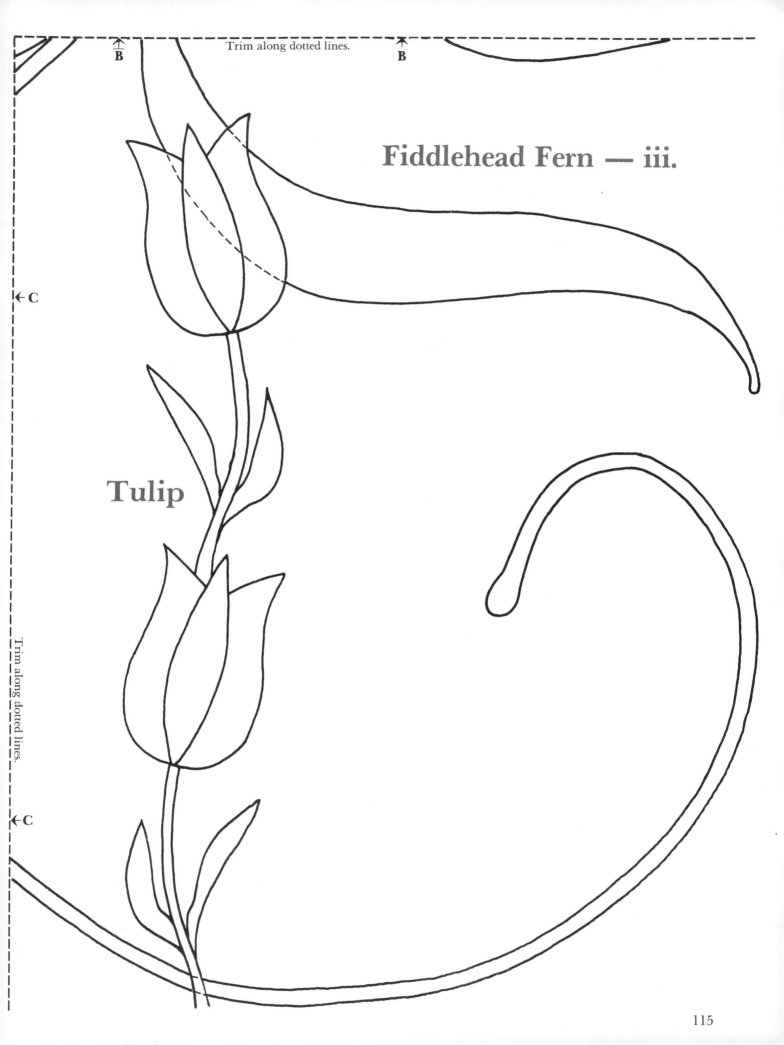

B

B

Fiddlehead Fern — iii.

C

Trim along dotted lines.

Tulip

C

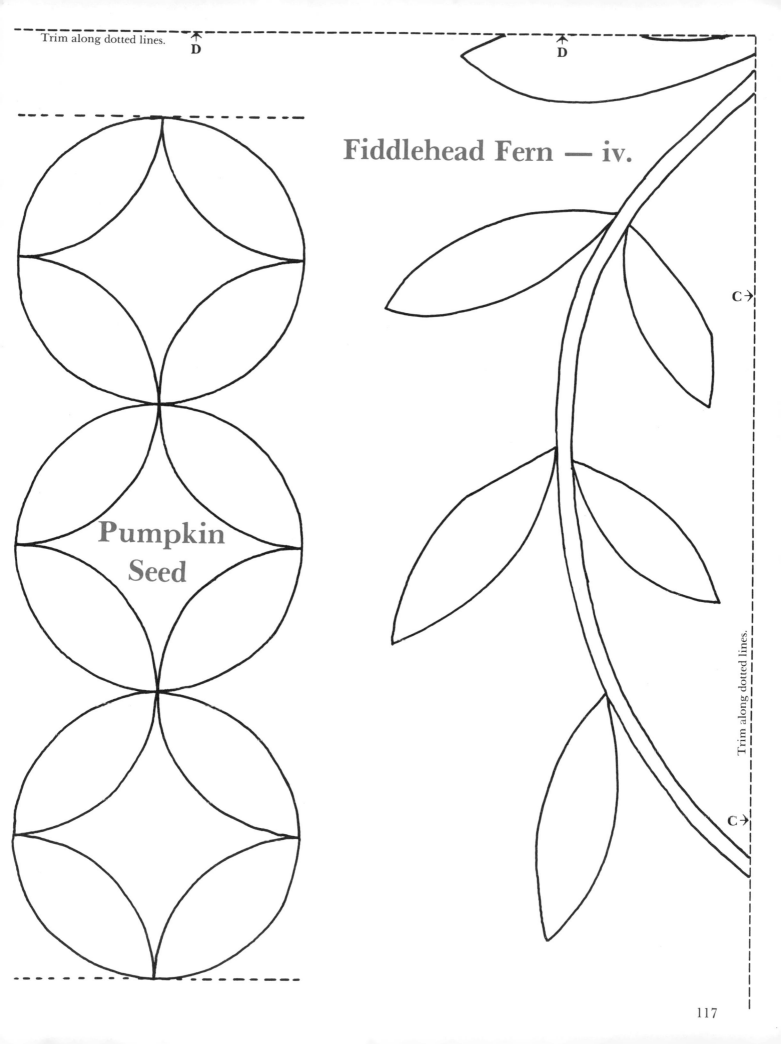

D

D

Fiddlehead Fern — iv.

C →

Pumpkin Seed

Trim along dotted lines.

C →

Cable — i.

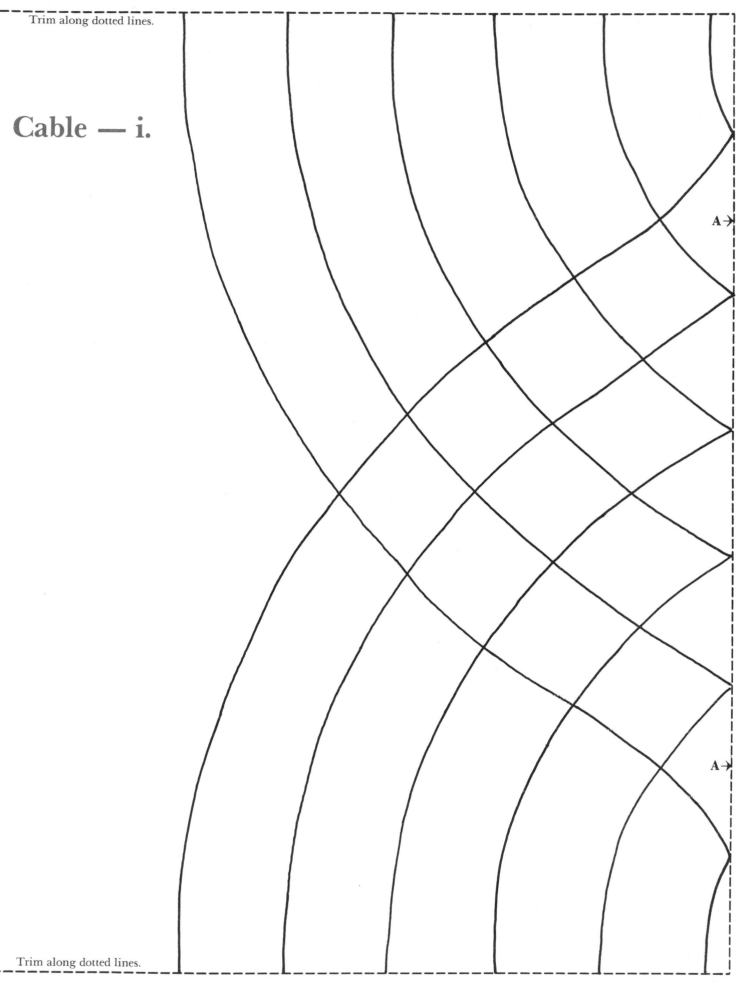

A→

A→

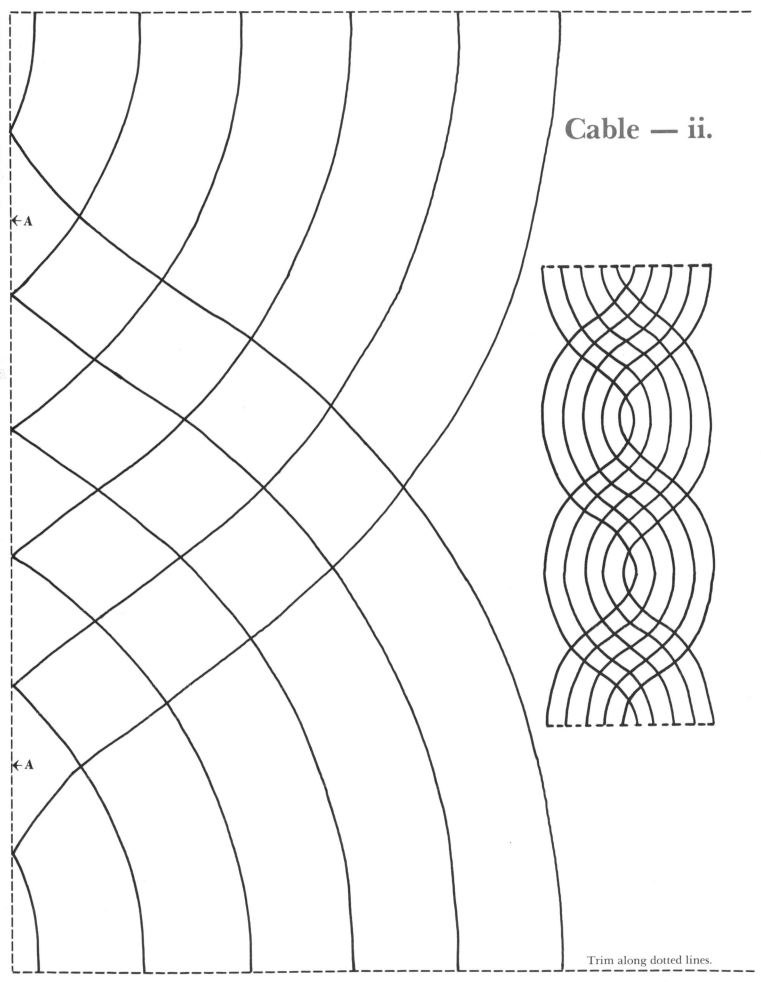

Cable — ii.

A

A

Trim along dotted lines.

Cable — iii.

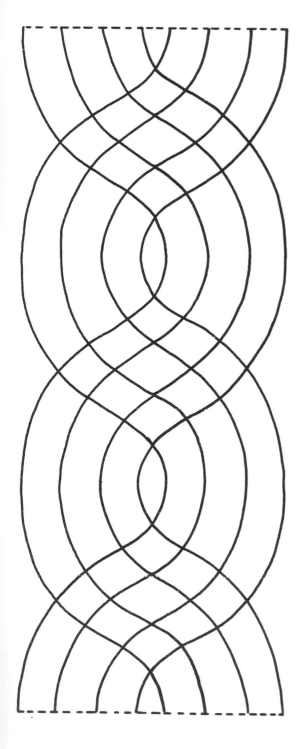
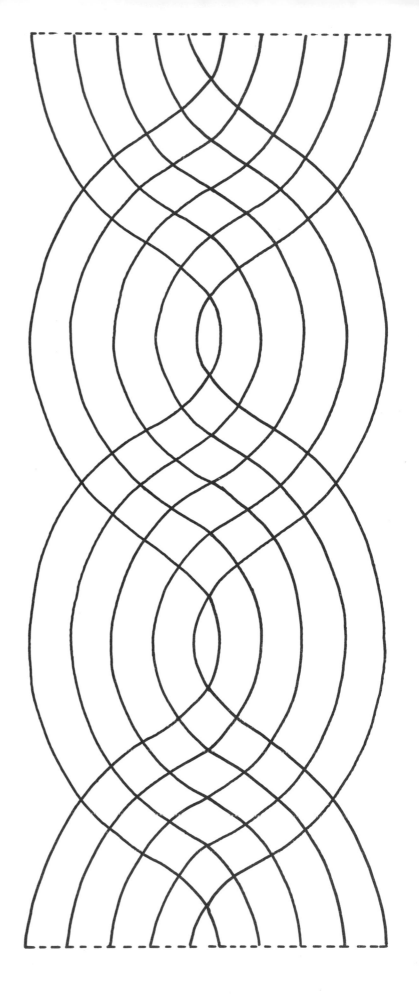

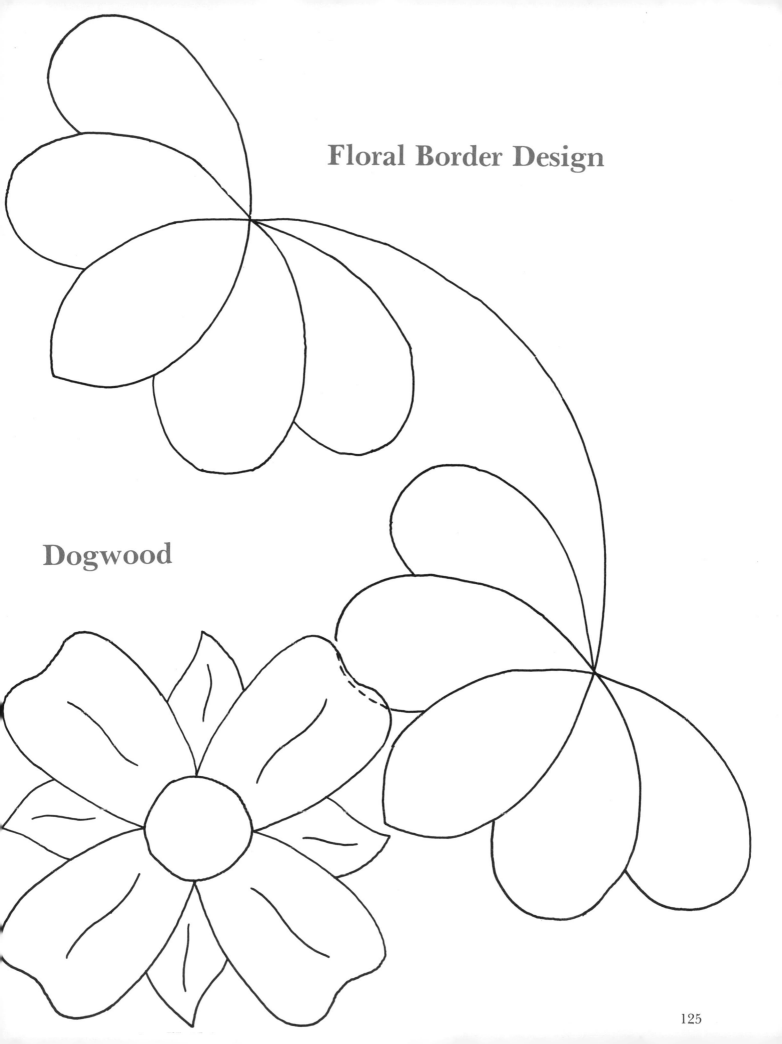

Floral Border Design

Dogwood

Readings and Sources

Cross Reference

Pellman, Rachel and Kenneth. **The World of Amish Quilts.** Good Books, Intercourse, Pennsylvania, 1984.

About Antique Amish Quilts

Bishop, Robert and Elizabeth Safanda. **A Gallery of Amish Quilts.** E. P. Dutton and Company, Inc., New York, New York, 1976.

Haders, Phyllis. **Sunshine and Shadow: The Amish and Their Quilts.** Universe Books, New York, New York, 1976.

Horton, Roberta. **Amish Adventure.** C & T Publishing. Lafayette, California, 1983.

Lawson, Suzy. **Amish Inspirations.** Amity Publications. Cottage Grove, Oregon, 1982.

Pottinger, David. **Quilts from the Indiana Amish.** E. P. Dutton, Inc., New York, New York, 1983.

About Other Quilts

Beyer, Jinny. **Patchwork Patterns.** EPM Publications, McLean, Virginia, 1979.

Danneman, Barbara. **Step by Step Quiltmaking.** Golden Press, Western Publishing Company, Inc., New York, New York, 1975.

Haders, Phyllis. **The Warner Collector's Guide to American Quilts.** The Main Street Press, New York, New York, 1981.

Hall, Carrie A. and Rose G. Kretsinger. **The Romance of the Patchwork Quilt in America.** Bonanza Books, New York, New York, 1935.

Hassel, Carla J. **You Can Be A Super Quilter!** Wallace-Homestead Book Company, Des Moines, Iowa, 1980.

Holstein, Jonathan. **The Pieced Quilt: An American Design Tradition.** New York Graphic Society, Boston, Massachusetts, 1973.

Houck, Carter and Myron Miller. **American Quilts and How To Make Them.** Charles Scribner's Sons, New York, New York, 1975.

Leone, Diana. **The Sampler Quilt.** Leone Publications, Santa Clara, California, 1980.

Murwin, Susan Aylsworth and Suzzy Chalfant Payne. **Quick and Easy Patchwork on the Sewing Machine.** Dover Publications, Inc., New York, New York, 1979.

Orlovsky, Patsy, and Myron Orlovsky. **Quilts in America.** McGraw Hill Book Company, New York, New York, 1974.

Pellman, Rachel T. and Joanne Ranck. **Quilts Among the Plain People.** Good Books, Intercourse, Pennsylvania. 1981.

About the Amish

Amish Cooking. Pathway Publishers, Aylmer, Ontario, 1965.

Bender, H. S. **The Anabaptist Vision.** Herald Press, Scottdale, Pennsylvania, 1967.

Braght, Thieleman J. van, Comp. **The Bloody Theatre; or, Martyrs Mirror.** Scottdale, Pennsylvania, 1951.

Budget, The. Sugarcreek, Ohio, 1890. A weekly newspaper serving the Amish and Mennonite communities.

Devoted Christian's Prayer Book. Pathway Publishing House, Aylmer, Ontario, 1967.

Family Life. Amish periodical published monthly. Pathway Publishing House, Aylmer, Ontario.

Gingerich, Orland. **The Amish of Canada.** Conrad Press. Waterloo, Ontario, 1972.

Good, Merle and Phyllis Pellman Good. **20 Most Asked Questions about the Amish and Mennonites.** Good Books, Lancaster, Pennsylvania, 1979.

Good, Phyllis Pellman and Rachel Thomas Pellman. **From Amish and Mennonite Kitchens.** Good Books, Intercourse, Pennsylvania, 1984.

Hostetler, John A. **Amish Life.** Herald Press, Scottdale, Pennsylvania, 1959.

Hostetler, John A. **Amish Society.** Johns Hopkins University Press, Baltimore, Maryland, 1963.

Keim, Albert N. **Compulsory Education and the Amish.** Beacon Press, Boston, Massachusetts, 1975.

Klaassen, Walter. **Anabaptism: Neither Catholic nor Protestant.** Conrad Press, Waterloo, Ontario, 1972.

Schreiber, William I. **Our Amish Neighbors.** University of Chicago Press, Chicago, Illinois, 1962.

Schweider, Elmer and Dorothy Schweider. **A Peculiar People: Iowa's Old Order Amish.** Iowa State University Press, Ames, Iowa, 1975.

Index

Amish, 6, 7
Amish colors, 9
Antique Amish quilts, 6

BACHELOR'S PUZZLE, 78
BARS, 22
BASKETS, 38
Batting, 14
BEAR PAW, 60
Binding, 14
Border, 10, 17
BOW TIE, 48
Broken Star, 34

Cable, 119
CAROLINA LILY, 56
CENTER DIAMOND, 18
Circular Feather, 83
Color, 8, 9, 10
Color wheel, 9
Colors, cool, 10
Colors, warm, 10
CROWN OF THORNS, 59

Diagonal Furrows (LOG CABIN variation), 28
DIAGONAL TRIANGLES, 71
Dogwood, 125
Double Four-Patch, 25
Double Irish Chain, 26
Double Nine-Patch, 24
DOUBLE T, 32

DOUBLE WEDDING RING, 68
DRUNKARD'S PATH, 72

Fabric, 8, 10
Fabric requirements, 10
Fabric selection, 9
FAN, 40
Feather Border, 99
Fiddlehead Fern, 111
Floral Border Design, 125
Frames, quilting, 14

GARDEN MAZE, 64
Grapes with Leaves, 109

IRISH CHAIN, 26
Ivy Leaf, 97

JACOB'S LADDER, 36

LOG CABIN, 28
Lone Star, 35

Marking, 11
Model, 8
MONKEY WRENCH, 54
MULTIPLE PATCH, 24

OCEAN WAVES, 42

Piecing, 11
    hand, 11
    machine, 12

PINWHEEL, 62
Pumpkin Seed, 87, 117

Quilting, 12-14
    frames, 14
    marking designs for, 12
    stitches, 12, 13

RAIL FENCE, 47
RAILROAD CROSSING, 66
ROBBING PETER TO PAY PAUL, 50
ROLLING STONE, 80
ROMAN STRIPE, 44

Sawtooth Diamond (CENTER DIAMOND variation), 19
Seam allowances, 10, 11, 12
SHOO-FLY, 53
Single Irish Chain, 27
STARS, 34
SUNSHINE AND SHADOW, 20

Templates, pattern, 11, 18-81
Templates, quilting, 83-125
TREE OF LIFE, 74
Triangular Rose, 89
Tulip, 115
TUMBLING BLOCKS, 46

Wild Goose Chase (BARS variation), 23

Yardage, 10

About the Author

Rachel Thomas Pellman is manager of The Old Country Store in Intercourse, Pennsylvania which features quilts, crafts, and toys made by more than 250 Amish and Mennonite craftspersons. A graduate of Eastern Mennonite College, she and her husband Kenneth have written THE WORLD OF AMISH QUILTS, a companion book to AMISH QUILT PATTERNS. She has also co-authored QUILTS AMONG THE PLAIN PEOPLE, FROM AMISH AND MENNONITE KITCHENS, and 12 Pennsylvania Dutch Cookbooks.

Rachel and Kenneth share an interest in folk art and crafts, and the interpretation of their people. Kenneth is manager of The People's Place, an educational center concerned with Amish and Mennonite arts, faith, and culture.

The Pellmans were married in 1976. They live in Lancaster, Pennsylvania, with their young son. They are members of the Rossmere Mennonite Church.